Dear Reader:

The book you are about to rea[...] Martin's True Crime Library, t[...] the *New York Times* calls "the leader in true crime!" Each month, we offer you a fascinating account of the latest, most sensational crime that has captured the national attention. St. Martin's is the publisher of bestselling true crime author and crime journalist Kieran Crowley, who explores the dark, deadly links between a prominent Manhattan surgeon and the disappearance of his wife fifteen years earlier in THE SURGEON'S WIFE. Suzy Spencer's BREAKING POINT guides readers through the tortuous twists and turns in the case of Andrea Yates, the Houston mother who drowned her five young children in the family's bathtub. In Edgar Award-nominated DARK DREAMS, legendary FBI profiler Roy Hazelwood and bestselling crime author Stephen G. Michaud shine light on the inner workings of America's most violent and depraved murderers. In the book you now hold, IF YOU REALLY LOVED ME, author Kevin F. McMurray tells the shocking story of two teenage lovers and the notorious murders of an elderly couple in Georgia, grandparents to one of the teens.

St. Martin's True Crime Library gives you the stories behind the headlines. Our authors take you right to the scene of the crime and into the minds of the most notorious murderers to show you what really makes them tick. St. Martin's True Crime Library paperbacks are better than the most terrifying thriller, because it's all true! The next time you want a crackling good read, make sure it's got the St. Martin's True Crime Library logo on the spine—you'll be up all night!

Charles E Spicer

Charles E. Spicer, Jr.
Executive Editor, St. Martin's True Crime Library

IF YOU REALLY REALLY LOVED ME

TWO TEENAGE GIRLS AND A SHOCKING DOUBLE MURDER

Kevin F. McMurray

St. Martin's Paperbacks

IF YOU REALLY LOVED ME

Copyright © 2006 by Kevin F. McMurray.

Cover photo of police line courtesy AP/Wide World Photos.
Portrait by REX USA.

All rights reserved. No part of this book may be used or reproduced in any manner whatsoever without written permission except in the case of brief quotations embodied in critical articles or reviews. For information address St. Martin's Press, 175 Fifth Avenue, New York, NY 10010.

ISBN: 0-312-93795-4
EAN: 9780312-93795-9

Printed in the United States of America

St. Martin's Paperbacks edition / May 2006

St. Martin's Paperbacks are published by St. Martin's Press, 175 Fifth Avenue, New York, NY 10010.

10 9 8 7 6 5 4 3 2 1

ACKNOWLEDGMENTS

The author is indebted to a multitude of sources in the research and writing of this book. He is particularly grateful to the murder victims' son, Kevin Collier, and the Fayette County Sheriff's Department, namely Sheriff Randall Johnson, lead investigator Lieutenant Colonel Bruce Jordan, and subordinates Lieutenant Tracey Carroll, Detectives Ethon Harper, Bo Turner, Phil McElwaney, and the Georgia Bureau of Investigation's Chief Medical Examiner Kris Sperry. Lawyers for the defense, Lloyd Walker and Judy Chidester, were extremely cooperative, as was District Attorney Scott Ballard and his office. The involved attorneys were informative and insightful.

Elizabeth and Tim Ketchum were generous in their relating of their family's history and the troubled life of their daughter Sandy Ketchum.

First Fayetteville Baptist Church's minister Glenn Stringham's earnest account of the lives of his good friends and the events surrounding the murders of Sarah and Carl Collier is much appreciated. Sara Polk's compelling story of her friendship with Sandy Ketchum and Holly Harvey, and the night of the murders was absolutely critical to the telling of this gripping story.

Patricia Pelleiren and her sons Brian Clayton and Brett Shremshock's tale of their unfortunate and trying involvement in this case was important—and I suspect cathartic—but nonetheless valued. Dodie Gay's contribution was also helpful to relating the story of the suspects' capture.

Expert commentary by forensic psychologists Geoffrey McKee, Lauren Woodhouse, Helen Smith and in particular criminal justice expert and psychology professor at Atlanta Christian College, Dr. Greg Moffatt, and professor of criminology at the University of South Florida's Dr. Kathleen Heide were all essential to comprehending the motives of juvenile criminal offenders and understanding the nature of their punishment.

I would also like to thank the Spalding County Sheriff's Department and the fine reporting of Fayette County's *The Citizen*, as well as *The Atlanta Journal-Constitution* and the Georgia Television Company d/b/a Atlanta's WSB-TV, on which I relied.

Sandy Ketchum's story of her sad life and the harrowing details of August 2, 2004, made this book poignant as well as riveting and relevant. Hopefully it will go far in the understanding of the mind of a teenage murderer. As usual my agent, Jane Dystel, did a terrific job with my interests at heart.

Lastly, special thanks to my daughter Kaitlyn for

her expert help in transcribing video and audio tapes. She speeded the process and the ease in the writing of this book immeasurably.

Kevin F. McMurray
November 2005

ONE

Reverend Glenn Stringham was home relaxing after a long day at his church on the evening of Monday, August 2, 2004, when his phone rang. He was used to fielding calls from members of the congregation even after church hours. Due to the age of his flock, calls continually came in regarding a sudden hospital emergency or yet another death. No clergyman in Fayette County, Georgia, presided over more funerals than he.

The urgent phone call came from a neighbor of his good friends Carl and Sarah Collier, who lived in the north end of the county in the residential community of Riverdale, not far from metropolitan Atlanta. The Colliers were not only friends, but active and valued members of his senior adults' congregation at the Fayetteville First Baptist Church. The neighbor told Stringham that there was a police car with its lights flashing outside the Collier home. Stringham knew that meant one thing: the Colliers were having trouble, again, with their granddaughter Holly.

Without giving it a second thought the 59-year-old

Baptist minister dialed the Colliers' home number, which he knew by heart. The answering machine picked up. Stringham wasn't surprised, surmising that they must be outside talking with the police officer. In his message he said that he knew they were having some "struggles," and if there was anything he could do, to not hesitate in calling him at home.

Within an hour Stringham got another call from the Colliers' neighbor. This time she was hysterical and blurted out that the elderly couple had been stabbed. Stringham said he would be right there.

Heading north up Route 314, the major thorough-fare from Fayetteville to the Hartsfield–Jackson Atlanta International Airport twenty miles distant, Stringham thought of the "struggles" that the Colliers had experienced of late.

He knew that they had taken 15-year-old Holly back into their home after a court appearance. Just last week they had accompanied her to juvenile court, where she was sentenced to probation after running away from the home of her mother's friend, where she had been staying. Stringham was afraid the youngster was head-ing down the same road as her mother Carla. It mysti-fied him that Carla, who was currently in jail for selling marijuana to an undercover policeman had come from such a fine home, the same home that Carla's older brother Kevin had flourished in. Kevin, a year and a half older than Carla, was a University of Georgia graduate and had a good job with Delta airlines. He was also a regular church-goer, and owned a comfort-able home just outside Fayetteville. Carla had dropped out of high school, was continually in trouble with the law, and had borne two children out of wedlock.

The Colliers had been very open with the problems they were having with their granddaughter. They had often consulted with Stringham and had asked their fellow congregants for their support and prayers.

Twenty-five minutes later, Stringham pulled up to the Colliers' modest ranch house on Plantation Drive. He could see that Fayette County Sheriff Randall Johnson was already there. Right then and there he knew the Colliers' neighbor had been right. Something terrible had happened.

Sheriff Johnson told his good friend Glen Stringham that Carl was dead on the kitchen floor and Sarah had been found in a pool of blood at the bottom of the basement steps, also dead. Johnson related to the stunned minister that there had been a horrific struggle and that there was blood everywhere. Stringham stood outside the Collier home as the crime-scene van arrived and detectives from the sheriff's department swarmed over the house. He learned from the sheriff what he himself had suspected. There was little doubt who had been responsible for the horrific act: Holly Harvey.

The Colliers' son Kevin should had been at work at the airport when he received a voice mail message on his cell phone at 8:30 PM, but he had gotten off early so he could attend orchestra practice at the First Baptist Church in the northern Atlanta suburb of Dunwoody. The rehearsal was for a dinner charity affair where they would be performing *The Sound of Music*. The voice on the message was Lisa Hargrove, a family friend who owned several houses with her husband Del in the Colliers' neighborhood.

The Hargroves had been checking out one of their houses, which was just across the street from Carl and Sarah's when they saw the patrol car. Like Glenn Stringham, the couple had thought that Holly must have been giving the Colliers problems again. Del had stepped into the carport and peered into the kitchen door window and seen Carl lying on the floor. One of the sheriff's deputies had observed him and warned him back. Del cautiously retreated to where his wife stood and told her what he'd seen. Lisa immediately called Kevin. She left a message on his voice mail that said there had been some "trouble" at his parents' place and for him to come home as soon as he could. When Kevin retrieved the message during a break, he dialed the cell number Lisa had given.

Lisa reiterated that there had been "some problems" at his parents' house and for him to come right over. Kevin asked whether it was an emergency, or if he could wait until rehearsal was over. She replied, "You should come now." Kevin said since he was all the way north in Dunwoody, it would take him at least an hour to get to the Riverdale house. On the drive south he called Lisa again. Kevin was worried and wanted more information. All Lisa would say was that it wasn't good, but Kevin persisted. He finally got it out of her that his dad was "hurt." He remembers that Lisa told him not to rush, which he thought was odd due to the apparent circumstances. Kevin stepped on the gas.

♦ ♦ ♦

Plantation Drive rises from Route 314 for about a quarter mile, until it crests, then drops down gently to where number 226 sits on the left side of the bucolic tree-lined street. Kevin Collier saw cops "everywhere." He remembers thinking "This *isn't* good." Pulling over, he noticed the crime-scene tape draped around the house and knew at that moment that both of his parents were gone. In stunned silence he surveyed the familiar surroundings. It seemed as if the entire neighborhood was out in the street gawking at the flashing police car lights and the uniformed men continually entering and exiting the split-level white brick ranch house that he had grown up in.

Sheriff Johnson was waiting for Kevin. The first words out of the mouth of the long-serving county sheriff were, "Remember how you saw them last."

Kevin blurted out that "Holly must have done this."

Looking around, he noticed his father's truck was gone. The police wouldn't let Kevin near the house. Staring at it, he could see figures moving about inside and camera flashes going off, giving the whole scene an eerie, surreal effect. Then he found himself being bombarded with questions from the police, especially in regards to his father's truck, a 2002 indigo blue Chevrolet Silverado.

In a state of shock he answered as best he could, continually muttering that "Holly must have done this."

TWO

Lieutenant Colonel Bruce Jordan is the director of investigations for the Fayette County Sheriff's Office. In the state of Georgia he has the reputation of being somewhat of a supercop. With a soft Southern drawl and a passing resemblance to former President Bill Clinton, the respected police detective also has a reputation for being single-minded in his pursuit of felons. The 44-year-old Jordan has his detractors, namely the local public defenders, who have complained that he has been too forthcoming with information about ongoing criminal cases. His "camera-friendly" reputation notwithstanding, nobody in the legal system or the media can argue with his success.

Jordan started as the nighttime radio operator with the sheriff's department in 1979 when he was just 19 years old and attending a local junior college. The young man impressed his superiors with his work ethic and proficiency and after just six months, he was offered a patrolman's job. He weighed the offer against the prospect of three more years of college and opted for the paycheck, telling himself he'd finish school at a later date. He never did, but his decision, Jordan would come to reflect, had been the right one.

Bruce Jordan's employment with the sheriff's department coincided with a population boom in Fayette County. It was an affluent populace that was in need of additional police protection. The county police department underwent massive changes in size as well as attitude, from an *Andy Griffith* type of mentality to a big city cop atmosphere. It was heady stuff for the hardworking Jordan. After just three years he was promoted to sergeant, then quickly detective sergeant and in 1988, division commander of detectives. In the summer of 2004, Bruce Jordan was lieutenant colonel, commanded forty detectives, and oversaw all criminal investigations, the K-9 corps, and the tactical division in the 250-man department. When the county decided to buy a helicopter for the sheriff's office, Jordan took a pilot's course and often flew it himself. When the department started a scuba diving unit, Jordan became certified, and took part in underwater searches for bodies and crime evidence. Bruce Jordan likes to think of himself as "a hands-on type of cop."

The once-rural Fayette County began inching up in murder rates as its population grew. Two reasons why Jordan is the longest sitting chief investigator for the sheriff's department are that during his term he personally worked every homicide, and that there is someone sitting in jail for committing each and every one of them. One murder prior to his employment, however, remained unsolved.

During 1977, the first year of Sheriff Randall Johnson's long tenure, Liddie Matthews Evans' partially decomposed body had been found floating in a portion of the Flint River that flowed through Fayette County. The cause of death was a gunshot wound.

In 1997 Jordan was researching what would be his first book, *Death Unexpected: The Violent Deaths of Fayette*, when he came across the case, which had become known as one of "the Flint River Murders." Jordan remembers thinking, "I believe I might be able to solve this case." In 2002 Jordan and Fayette County Sergeant Tracey Carroll went back and not only unraveled the mysterious homicide in their jurisdiction, but also the four other unsolved murder cases in adjoining counties. It was a compelling story of betrayal and murder.

Carl Patton Jr. had been a strong-arm for his uncle, Fred Wyatt, a notoriously brutal Atlanta drug trafficker. Curiously, Wyatt had spread the word that his hulking nephew was a hit man to intimidate customers who were in payment arrears—as if Wyatt's clientele didn't already live in fear of him.

Ironically a woman by the name of Marie Jackson Wyatt, who was Fred Wyatt's common-law wife hired Carl to kill his uncle in 1977. It wasn't the first time she had employed the services of Carl Patton. In 1973 she'd had him kill her first husband, Richard Russell Jackson.

Marie Wyatt had wanted her second husband dead ever since he had left her for another woman, Betty Jo Ephlin. At Marie's behest, he had killed Betty Jo, but Patton was reluctant to kill his uncle. Finally out of fear for his own life, Patton, knowing that his uncle suspected him in the murder of his girlfriend, shot Wyatt in the head during a purported hunting trip. He placed Wyatt's body in his Volkswagen Rabbit and ran it into a moving train in Clayton County to conceal his crime. As it would turn out, it was a sloppy cover-up attempt. The crime-scene photo of the wreck clearly showed a bullet hole in Wyatt's head.

One month later Patton further covered his murderous trail by shooting Liddie Matthews Evans and her boyfriend Joe Cleveland to death in Patton's DeKalb County trailer home. Apparently Patton was afraid that Matthews and Cleveland had information that could link Patton to the deaths of Fred Wyatt and Betty Jo Ephlin.

It was a twisted trail of murders where all the bodies, except his uncle's, were dumped in the Flint River.

Bruce Jordan and Tracey Carroll spent four months tracking down potential witnesses. They also found mention of a piece of evidence in the twenty-five-year-old case files: a bloody cushion that had been found in a camper in Carl Patton's backyard. In 1977 Patton's property had been searched, since he had been a suspect in the murders.

Back in the 1970s, before effective DNA forensic testing, all that could be determined from the stain was the blood type. The two detectives believed that if they could find that cushion, they could link it to the floater, Liddie Matthews Evans, through DNA. Jordan and Carroll got the unusual permission of Clayton County's chief of police to search the department's evidence room. Within ten minutes they found the cushion. Liddie Matthews Evans' body was exhumed in Alabama and transported back to Atlanta. Due to the age and decomposition of the corpse, the medical examiners were only able to get a partial DNA profile, but Jordan and Carroll tracked down the victim's children. Their profiles of the victim matched the ones lifted from the bloody cushion.

By this time, Patton was living two counties over from Fayette in Henry County, with his wife and his grandchildren, who had been deserted by their parents. Jordan had the home staked out by his sniper team to observe Patton's movements and whether he was accustomed to carrying a firearm. The Fayette County detectives then paid the Pattons a late night visit. They were separated for interrogation and Jordan explained the situation to the mum wife, Norma J. Patton. He told her that if she had helped with the murders, "she should keep quiet," but if all she'd done was help hide bodies, then she "had better talk" to him. Jordan then threw a color photo of the body of the victim on the table. Liddie Matthews Evans had been raped and mutilated after death. The crime-scene photo showed the water-logged corpse dressed in slacks with her vagina exposed. Jordan told Norma that semen had been found in the vaginal cavity. He then tried a ruse. He told Norma they had a DNA match that proved it was her husband's semen. Jordan asked her if she had known what her husband had done to the body. While the woman studied the grisly photo, she quietly shook her head from side to side. Jordan said that he believed her. Patton's wife, in a whisper, finally said, "All I did was help hide bodies."

Carl Patton Jr. was eventually connected to all five

murders. He confessed and got five consecutive life sentences without the chance of parole.

Bruce Jordan thought that would be the last he would ever hear of the serial murderer. But Patton would later surprise Jordan with a phone call and a strange request. He had seen the Fayette County lawman on the TV news long before his arrest, thinking at the time that if he ever saw that face in person, he knew he "was done." After telling Jordan that, he then asked a favor. He said he had a daughter who had been missing two and a half years, adding, "And I didn't kill her." He wanted Jordan to apply the same diligence he'd used in capturing him towards finding his lost daughter. Jordan agreed to look into the disappearance. He found her three days later.

Jordan, after making an inquiry to the Fulton County Medical Examiner's office in Atlanta, learned that they had an unidentified dismembered body on their hands. The medical examiners had determined it was the body of a Caucasian male. Apparently they questioned their own findings after Jordan inquired about the unidentified corpse. The second re-examination suggested otherwise. Jordan received a tip from an inside source telling him of the misidentification. He called and demanded an explanation. According to Jordan, the coroner tried to keep it secret that they had been mistaken. It was an embarrassing lapse by the big city morgue. Through DNA, the body was identified as Carl Patton's daughter, Melissa Wolfenberger.

The woman's husband Christopher Wolfenberger was later arrested on unrelated charges. There would be no thanks coming Jordan's way from the Atlanta

Police Department and the Fulton County Medical Examiner's office. The detective from the suburban Fayette County Sheriff's Department had made both his big city counterparts look incompetent. Jordan also was hung with the tag of being a "showboater," a slight he would continue to hear repeatedly after the events of August 2, 2004.

On the night of August 2, the Fayette County Sheriff's Office received a call from the neighboring Spalding County Sheriff's Office. Their 911 dispatcher had gotten a report at 6:14 PM from the parents of a teenage girl by the name of Sara Polk that two of her friends had shown up at their house in Griffin "all bloody," saying that they had just been mugged and wanted to clean up. The two girls were friends of Sara's, Holly Harvey and Sandy Ketchum. Minutes later, Sara would relate, Holly boasted that she and Sandy Ketchum had actually just killed Holly's grandparents. Holly and Sandy left the house telling Sara to "be sure and watch the news on television tonight."

The Spalding County Sheriff's Office couldn't locate anyone by the name of the purported victims residing in their jurisdiction. They instructed Sara Polk to call her friend on her cell phone and ask for the names and address of her grandparents so she could make sure if the deaths were reported on the TV news. Holly gave her the information. The Clayton County sheriff's dispatcher then called the Fayette sheriff's department and directed them to Carl and Sarah Collier's house on 226 Plantation Drive.

At 7:35 PM Spalding County 911 contacted Fayette

County 911 and requested a welfare check on the couple. At 7:42 Fayette County 911 dispatched Deputies David Martin and Mike James, who arrived at the Riverdale address seconds apart.

Martin pulled into the driveway with his lights flashing. Emerging from his patrol car, he walked past the carport and looked around the corner of the building, seeing nothing suspicious. Martin and James then began to check the home, looking through some partially open blinds on the carport door. Martin could see an elderly white male lying face down with both his head and upper body surrounded by a pool of coagulated blood. He appeared not to be breathing. Martin also noticed that a white wall phone was lying inches from the body's right hand.

Martin and James entered the home through the unlocked kitchen door. Once inside, Martin noticed Del Hargrove approaching the kitchen/carport door. Martin advised Hargrove to back away from the house as James continued to check it. James found the stairway door that led to the basement and opened it. Partially down the staircase he could see a white female lying face up in a large pool of dried blood. James could see wounds on the subject's chest, and that "she was clearly deceased." James advised the sheriff's HQ of the second victim at 7:46 PM. Both deputies then exited the house to await the arrival of EMS, supervisors, and investigators.

While waiting outside they were informed by Hargrove that Collier's granddaughter, Holly Harvey, was also a resident of 226 Plantation Drive. While standing in front of the white brick ranch house, Martin watched as Deputies Clark Vickery and Thomas Mindar pulled up in their squad cars. The four sheriff's deputies conferred and decided that crime-scene protocol called for them to re-enter the house and search for other residents or suspects.

The ground level, the upstairs of the house, was empty. They proceeded down the stairs to search the finished basement.

After carefully stepping around the body of Sarah Collier, they found the downstairs splattered with blood. They found a small dog cowering in a corner. Deputy Mindar picked up the terrified animal, unlocked and opened the sliding glass door, and put it outside. His fellow officers followed him out, not wanting to contaminate the crime scene, since there was little they could do for the victims.

Minutes later Lieutenant Tom Brenna pulled up in front of the house and was briefed by Deputy Mindar. Brenna retrieved a roll of crime-scene tape from the trunk of his unmarked car and instructed Mindar to secure the property. As he approached the residence, he was met by Deputies Martin and James, and advised of the discovery and location of the two bodies.

Martin led Lieutenant Brenna to the kitchen door inside the carport, where he observed that Carl Collier's body had lost "an incredible amount of blood." Martin then led him to the staircase to the basement where he immediately saw the body of Sarah Collier, who had also lost a lot of blood. Brenna then left the residence through the same kitchen entrance, making sure he touched nothing.

EMS arrived on the scene and Brenna told them there was nothing they could do for the victims.

At 7:47 PM Fayette County Sheriff's Detective Ethon Harper arrived. He was directed by the waiting deputies to the carport door, where he could clearly see the white male lying on the kitchen floor. He noticed the detached phone beside him.

Harper then walked around the carport and the corner of the house to the backyard. There was a steep drop-off to the rear of the home. The house was deceptively roomy. The backyard was cut away, exposing a finished basement framed by a sliding glass door, which opened up to a slate patio area cluttered with a barbecue grill, a small child's bicycle, and stacked lumber. To the right of the door there was a stone retaining wall that stood a good five feet high. To the left of the door was an open area affording a view from a basement bedroom to an airy backyard that led gradually up to an aboveground pool.

The tall detective peered in through the sliding glass door where he observed the white female lying on her back at the foot of a staircase with blood all around her. He also noticed what appeared to be blood on the white walls in the interior of the basement. The accompanying deputies advised the detective that the victim was dead. Harper called his immediate supervisor, Sergeant Carroll, and advised her of what he'd found.

At 8:30 PM Sergeant Detective Tracey Carroll, Lieutenant Colonel Bruce Jordan, Crime Scene Investigator Gwen Graham, and Lieutenant Tray Powell arrived and entered the Collier residence with Detective Harper.

They had put on protective gloves and shoe covers so as not to contaminate the crime scene.

Inside the kitchen area they studied the prone body of Carl Collier. Collier was shoeless, his feet clad in white socks. He wore blue jeans and a white T-shirt. He was surrounded by a large amount of blood. The three detectives also noticed blood spatter on the cabinets, countertops, appliances, and the island area of the kitchen. It was obvious that a violent struggle had taken place here. In all his years of police work, Jordan had never seen anything this horrific, and he had seen plenty. He could only shake his head. It was incomprehensible to him that such a vicious attack could be launched on such an elderly pair—especially by a family member, which, from what he'd been told by the early arriving deputies, was likely the case.

After passing through the kitchen they checked each of the three upstairs bedrooms and found them undisturbed. There appeared to be no signs of forced entry into the home.

When they entered the living area just off the kitchen, Jordan noticed a bloody footprint on the carpet. The small print appeared to be pointed as if the person had exited the kitchen near Carl Collier's head and walked toward the basement stairway. Graham photographed the stairway and small amounts of blood on the handrail.

As the foursome descended the staircase they could immediately see the body of Sarah Collier lying on her back, feet pushed against the carpeted floor and her knees lifted. She was surrounded by a voluminous amount of blood. She was wearing a gaily patterned shirt and shorts, no doubt in preparation for her up-coming Hawaiian trip. The shirt was ripped open, exposing one severe laceration to her chest. Like her husband, she was shoeless, wearing only white socks. Her eyeglasses still sat on the bridge of her nose. Her eyes were open and she had a "horrified expression" on her lifeless face. Jordan instructed Graham to photograph the body.

From the bottom of the stairs they entered into an open living/storage area with outside access through a sliding glass door. On the wall next to the door they saw more smeared blood and blood spatter. A struggle, the four detectives concluded, had ensued here as well. On the floor next to the door they observed a wall phone with the cord cut.

The blood on the floor appeared to lead down a hallway to another bedroom, this one in the basement. Just inside the entryway, Jordan spotted a broken pair of eyeglasses on the floor. The three turned their attention to the disheveled bedding. It was covered in blood. The bedroom reeked with the distinctive odor of marijuana. This, Jordan thought, is where it all started.

On the bed was also some broken glass that contained seashells that appeared to be part of a lamp. Curiously the detectives also discovered cuts in the bed caused by a knife. There were no bloodstains around these. A picture on the wall depicting a litter of white puppies had similar cuts through it, without any damage to the wall behind. The picture, the detectives surmised, must have been placed on the bed and stabbed, causing the cuts to the picture and sheet, and then returned to its spot on the wall. Half of a sandwich with one bite taken out of it sat on the bedroom dresser.

The remaining areas of the basement were checked out, but no signs of any struggle were found. There was also no sign of forced entry on the sliding glass door. At 9:00 PM Bruce Jordan asked to have the coroner notified. Crime Scene Investigators Manny Rojas and Josh Shelton had joined Graham and begun documenting everything inside and outside the house on film. Powdering for latent fingerprints also commenced.

Detective Harper exited the house and began interviewing Kevin Collier. Kevin told the detective that his father's Chevrolet Silverado was missing. He also said his sister, Carla Harvey, mother of Holly, was currently serving time in jail, and that his parents had been having a difficult time taking care of Holly. Just last week, she had threatened them, he told Harper.

While speaking with Kevin, Tracey Carroll approached the pair holding a stack of photos that had been found in Holly's bedroom. The pictures had one thing in common: they were candid and posed shots taken at the beach. Kevin identified his niece in many of them.

The address on Plantation Drive was vaguely familiar to the tall, soft-spoken detective. From his cell phone he placed a call to his friend and fellow detective Bo Turner.

Turner was with his wife and kids looking at a house they were considering buying. Harper asked him if the 226 Plantation Drive address rang a bell. Turner said it sounded familiar, but he couldn't place it. Harper informed Turner of what had happened there. Bo Harper told Turner that he would be right over. Minutes later as he turned onto Plantation Drive from Route 314 and climbed the hill, it came to him—Holly Harvey.

Turner, just a couple of weeks before, had responded to a juvenile complaint at this very address with his regular partner Detective Phil McElwaney. The facts of the case and the runaway teenager came back to him. The stocky, shaven-headed detective remembered how he and McElwaney, working out of the juvenile division, had sifted through Holly's small circle of friends and then paid a visit to the home of Sandra Ketchum in Griffin. Sure enough, that was where the two detectives found Holly Harvey. They had notified the Fayetteville police that they'd found her, and the department sent two detectives trained to deal with teenage runaways.

Bo Turner never ceased to be amazed how well Bruce Jordan could take command of a seemingly chaotic situation and exert control and order over it. The crime scene took on the feeling of a military operation. Jordan's mind was working in dozens of directions and he instructed his deputies and detectives accordingly. He had Bo Turner and Phil McElwaney drive down to the Spalding County Sheriff's Office in Griffin. The department there had brought Sara Polk in for questioning.

THREE

Carl Collier came from the small, rural, northern Georgia town of Cartersville where he was the youngest of seven children. It was in high school where he met Sarah Jenkins. Almost two years younger than he, Sarah was playing for the girls' basketball team when she caught his eye. He was a cheerleader on the sideline. Carl asked if he could give her a ride home after the game, but Sarah politely refused the brash offer from the tall and handsome cheerleader. Carl, not to be so quickly brushed off, asked for a phone number, but the pretty young girl refused him again. She was not being coy. Young Sarah lived in a two-room house that did not even have a party phone line. In rural Georgia, even in the late 1940s, a telephone was a luxury only the well-off could afford, and Sarah Jenkins' family certainly would not be described as "well-off." Both her parents worked at a local mill, earning just enough to support themselves and Sarah and an older brother.

Persistence paid off for Carl Collier. After several requests for a date, Sarah finally said yes. A steady relationship developed and the couple married not long after Sarah graduated from high school. She was 19 and Carl was 21. Shortly after their wedding Carl joined the army and served stateside during the Korean conflict.

After the stint in the army Carl got a job at a Ford automobile assembly plant in Atlanta, then a position with the US Army Corps of Engineers before finally landing a job with Delta airlines in 1955. Delta was undergoing phenomenal growth in the 1950s with the advent of jet travel, and getting a mechanic's position with the up-and-coming airline was considered quite a coup for an ambitious young man. Like many of his fellow employees at Delta, Carl prospered. He rose to the position of manager of the power plant at the Delta maintenance depot. The couple was not blessed with children of their own, so they adopted a baby boy they named Kevin in 1965 and a baby girl, Carla, in 1967.

With a good income and a desire to raise their children in a better environment, the Colliers decided to move out of the city and bought a home just south of the ever-expanding Hartfield–Jackson Atlanta International Airport in Fayette County. The home was just twenty minutes from work, but the countrified, leafy neighborhood was a world away. It was an ideal setting to raise a family: a solid middle-class neighborhood full of hard-working, church-going people.

The Colliers were "model parents" and "as good of parents as anyone could have hoped for" according to son Kevin. They never kept it secret that their kids were adopted, and it was never an issue, says Kevin. They were always involved in what their children did.

They never stood in their way and always let them do what they needed to do to pursue their dreams, but the two children couldn't have been more different.

Kevin excelled in school and showed a gift for music, which was encouraged and nurtured by his parents. Carla, a year and a half younger, was, although bright, an indifferent student and showed no inclination to further her musical talents other than the obligatory piano lessons.

The Colliers were concerned and diligent parents. They always made it their business to find out about their children's friends, and even learn everything they could about the parents of the friends. They believed a child's background and upbringing determined character, and they didn't want their children led astray by problem peers.

Church was important to the Colliers and they tried to transplant their devotion to their Baptist faith by seeing that Kevin and Carla were regular attendees at the Fayetteville First Baptist Church, where they were in the youth choir. And, of course, there was the compulsory church-sponsored Sunday school.

When Kevin showed a keen aptitude for music, the Colliers began attending the First Baptist Church Atlanta, an hour's drive from their Fayette County home. First Baptist had an outstanding musical education program and was known throughout the South for its full ensemble orchestra. Kevin excelled in the program and his parents traveled all over the country and abroad to proudly hear their son play. Kevin would later gain all-state honors for his musical ability and would be offered a music scholarship to the University of Georgia in Athens.

Carla's adolescence, however, was a bit more problematic. Kevin relates that he and his sister had a normal brother–sister relationship, describing it as "loving one another one moment, and hating each other the next." When Kevin left for the University of Georgia, a couple of hours away in Athens, things got worse between his sister and his parents.

The Colliers did not approve of Carla's friends in high school, and she began to challenge her parents' authority. On visits home Kevin watched in horror as his parents got in "knock-down, drag-out fights" with Carla. Most of the problems stemmed from the crowd she had begun to hang out with at school.

In the tenth grade, at the age of 15, Carla dropped out of school and ran off with a boyfriend. The two young lovers went on a coast-to-coast jaunt, ending up in California. The young man's name was Gene Harvey, but on their cross-country romp he had stolen the identity of his girlfriend's brother.

Carla had provided Harvey with Kevin's Social Security number. Harvey was then able to get drivers' licenses in Kevin's name. Gene Harvey was in jail when Kevin found out about the identity theft. Harvey was jailed under the name of Kevin Collier on January 8, 1988. On September 4, 1988, the 27-year-old Harvey was convicted of "impersonating another" in Gwinnett County and sentenced to a year in jail. It took almost that long for Kevin Collier to clear his name with the help of a lawyer.

Back home in Georgia, Carla moved in with Gene Harvey in a house thirty miles south of Fayetteville. By this time Carla's parents had resigned themselves to the fact that Carla was out of their control. The Colliers found support and solace in their deep and abiding faith, and were considered staunch members of their church.

Glenn Stringham recalled how, when you met Carl and Sarah Collier, you became their friend. The gentle couple never had a cross word with anyone. Stringham said the Colliers were always the first two to arrive for a church mission or outing no matter what time of day it was. Stringham remembers fondly how, whenever he brought the church bus around, often before the sun was up, in preparation for another trip, Carl and Sarah would be there waiting. The first words out of their mouths were "What can we do to help?"

Stringham was proud to be their pastor. The couple would later sing in the senior adult choir and they both ministered side by side in many of the missions the church sponsored. According to Stringham, the Colliers were church leaders.

A mission trip to North Dakota was a good example of what a fine Christian Carl Collier was. Fayetteville First Baptist often took volunteers to needy areas of the country and assisted the local churches in whatever tasks needed to be done. Sarah, because of her job at a local bank, couldn't take the time off, but Carl, retired from Delta, yet busy with his painting business, did. He spent a month with Glen Stringham and thirty-three others building a church for the remote rural community from the concrete slab up. Collier, now in his seventies, worked long hours tirelessly to help build that church without a nickel in compensation. His reward, says Stringham, was knowing that he was helping others.

On March 23, 1989, Carla gave birth to a healthy baby girl she named Holly. Gene Harvey was listed on the birth certificate as the father. Carla had told her parents and brother that they had married, but neither Kevin nor his parents believed it. It was not in Carla's nature to observe such social niceties as matrimony. Carla and Holly took Harvey as the family name.

When Holly was just 18 months old, the family was involved in a car accident that left Gene Harvey a paraplegic. The marriage did not hold up under the strains of Gene's handicap. Carla eventually took Holly and moved in with her parents on Plantation Drive.

Carl and Sarah were just happy to have Carla back, and overjoyed to have their adorable granddaughter under the same roof with them. But maturity and motherhood had not mellowed Carla. She would continually leave her daughter in her aging parents' care while she went out to clubs and bars, often not returning home at night. The Colliers loved Holly, even doted on her, but Carl and Sarah were retired and wanted to relax, travel, and enjoy the fruits of their labor. A second parenthood was not what they'd had in mind. Battles over Carla's lack of responsibility ensued. Exasperated, the Colliers told Carla that she and Holly would have to move out.

Carla got an apartment over in Clayton County and a gig as a stripper at a local club. When she was unable to find someone to baby-sit while she was at work—

which was often—she would drop Holly off at her parents' home. The Colliers never refused the little girl. She was their granddaughter. They loved her and were worried about her upbringing.

In 1993 the senior Colliers were relieved when Carla, with 4-year-old Holly in tow, moved in with Kevin in his newly purchased home in an attractive subdivision on the outskirts of Fayetteville. Maybe, they hoped, a stable environment for Holly would result. That was not to be.

Kevin remembers his sister's total unwillingness to discipline the child. Holly was given free rein in the household. Kevin could only shake his head, since his sister was not inclined to getting lessons in parenthood from her bachelor brother. Holly called her mother by her first name. It was a clear sign to Kevin that she had no respect for her mother, and, he says, there was no structured environment for Holly: no bedtime, no wake-up time, and no school departure time. According to Kevin, the only time Holly had a structured environment was when she stayed with her grandparents.

By 2001 Carla had racked up three DWIs (Driving While Intoxicated, twice with Holly in the car, convictions), and spent five months in jail. Holly continued to stay with her uncle and by this time was old enough to be left at home alone. Kevin recalls that the time her mother was away in jail was "great." Kevin had restored some order in her life. She was thriving, and getting along just fine with her uncle. Carla was eventually let out of jail on probation and rejoined her brother and daughter at Kevin's home. The disjointed family life quickly deteriorated again.

One night, pulling into his garage after a day's work, Kevin was met at the door by Holly. She was in tears. She told him that she and her mother had a spat. Confronting his sister, an argument ensued, followed by fisticuffs. The police were called. The "domestic dispute" was the last straw for Kevin. He threw both his sister and niece out of his house. Carla and Holly were just too much of a disruptive force in his life.

On April 2, 2003, Carla got into trouble once again. This time it was for distribution of narcotics. She had been busted for selling marijuana to an undercover police officer. Carla quickly found herself back in the county jail on April 29th, looking at a 3-year stretch.

Holly moved in with the family of a friend, Haley Earwood, who lived nearby in Conyers. Her mother, Connie Earwood, worked at a school over in Flat Rock where, for convenience's sake, Holly was enrolled in the middle school. It was there that Holly met and became best friends with Sandy Ketchum.

On June 6, 2004, Kevin Collier got a phone call from Holly asking if she and a friend could come over to his house. Kevin told her he had no problem with it, and told his niece it would be nice to see her. Holly, with Sandy in tow, arrived early the next morning. Kevin had never met Sandy before. He couldn't help noticing that the 5'4", brown-haired, brown-eyed girl dressed like a boy and didn't talk much. Kevin had to run out of the house and take care of some errands, and when he returned at 11:30 AM, both girls were gone. Kevin drove around the neighborhood and found no sign of the two. He waited for a while at home for their return, but finally called his parents' house to see if Holly and her friend had paid them a visit.

Kevin's mother went "ballistic" and was "outraged" that her son had let the Ketchum girl spend time with Holly. Unbeknownst to him, Sandy Ketchum was not permitted over at the Collier residence, and they had told Mrs. Earwood over in Conyers that they wanted their wishes regarding Sandy respected there too. The Colliers knew about Sandy's troubled childhood and her father's numerous wives. The 16-year-old friend was a bad influence on Holly. They sternly told their son that Sandy was never to be permitted to visit Holly again. When the conversation ended, Carl Collier dialed the Fayette County Sheriff's Office.

Detective Phil McElwaney took the call. Carl told the policeman that his granddaughter had run away, and that she'd had a problem with drugs in the past and may be using them again. After getting a description of the 110-pound, 5'6", brown-haired, blue-eyed Holly and a list of her friends, McElwaney and his partner Detective Bo Turner made several calls over the next three days. It was a call they got on June 9 that looked to be the best lead. Tim Ketchum was notifying the police that his daughter Sandy was missing, and one of the numbers she had called the day she disappeared was to Holly Harvey's cell phone. Ketchum told the detectives his daughter might have headed for her natural mother's house in Griffin.

On June 11 McElwaney and Turner drove down to Griffin to check on an address where they had learned that the mother of Sandy Ketchum lived.

Holly was in the ramshackle house when the two

detectives arrived. Once they identified her, they
placed a call to the Fayetteville Police Department and
arranged for Detective Debbie Chambers to transport
Holly back to Fayetteville. Sandy, since she was with
her mother, stayed put. Back in Fayetteville the sullen
teen was turned over to her waiting grandfather, Carl
Collier.

Holly's reception at home by her grandmother was
chilly. Carl kept his anger in check, but lectured his
granddaughter about her attitude and her irresponsible
actions of late. He also told the mute teen that he, her
grandmother, and her uncle had been worried about
her. Holly skulked down to her basement room.

On July 2, Kevin Collier got a call from Holly. She
asked if she and Sandy could spend the weekend of the
Fourth at his place in Fayetteville. Kevin wasn't too
keen on the idea, remembering the last time she'd been
over in early June. Besides, Holly was supposed to be
spending the weekends with her grandparents. Holly
pleaded with her uncle, complaining how much she
hated staying with them. Kevin had known she was
miserable there, and finally agreed to her staying at his
place, after he got her assurances that there would be
no trouble.

Kevin couldn't see what his mom's concern was
about in regard to Sandy Ketchum. Even if she'd come
from a broken home, hadn't Holly? His sister—
Holly's mother—was a divorced single mom, a stripper and a convicted felon. Hell, he thought, Carla was
now sitting in a jail cell. It was hardly an endorsement
of Holly's family background, and backgrounds

seemed to matter so much to his mom. It was a case of the pot calling the kettle black to Kevin Collier. He had no intention of mentioning the weekend stay-over to his mom. What she didn't know couldn't hurt her.

Sandy, again, was "real quiet" and Kevin had to "dig stuff out of her," but otherwise she seemed nice enough, although she did appear to be a tomboy. In retrospect, Kevin Collier admitted he hadn't "put two and two together." Their strong attachment seemed a little over the top, but he had just written it off as "kids being kids." As far as he was concerned, it was just two teenage girlfriends hanging out together.

Kevin would learn how close the teenagers were when his live-in girlfriend Sandra Adams spelled it out for him. Holly had opened up to Sandra and told her that she and Sandy were lesbian lovers. Sandra had pretty much figured it out anyway from observing the pair. After being told, Kevin was shocked and at a loss as what to do about it. As a 37-year-old bachelor uncle, there was little he could do. Holly still had a mother, albeit in jail, a legal guardian in Connie Earwood, and concerned grandparents. Kevin decided to keep his nose out of it.

FOUR

Tim Ketchum started going out with Sandra Faye when he was 24 years old in 1987. Sandra Faye, 19 years of age was pretty, friendly, and several years younger. She was also divorced with two children. It wasn't long after the initial courtship that Sandra got pregnant. She gave birth to a healthy girl on April 19, 1988. They named her after her mother, but to keep the confusion to a minimum, they agreed to call the baby Sandy. Shortly after the birth, Tim "did the right thing" and the couple married. A truck driver, Tim knew it would be hard to support a family, but he was determined to make an effort at it.

Problems began almost immediately. Sandra didn't pay much attention to her two kids or her baby girl, leaving her in soiled diapers and hungry most of the time. She was more interested in going out at night and sleeping in late.

Family & Children Services got involved. They were threatening to take Sandy away because of Sandra's problems with her two children from her previous marriage. The social worker was at their home checking on the other two children, and noticed that Sandy needed to have her diaper changed. Sandra refused to do it. After insisting she must, Sandra finally complied and the social worker was alarmed that Sandy had a severe case of diaper rash.

Once, when Tim's sister Glenda stopped by to pick up Sandy, her mother could not tell her where Sandy's formula, spare diapers, and clothing were, and refused to help her sister-in-law look for them. Sandra, said her sister-in-law, fell across her bed and acted like she was crying. Tim's sister noted no tears flowed. When Glenda got the 1-year-old home, she was shocked by the severity of Sandy's diaper rash, and immediately took the child to a doctor.

Tim constantly battled with his young wife over her lack of attention to the baby. When he found out that Sandra had been deserting Sandy and "running around on him" while he was at work, he decided enough was enough. He threw Sandra out and she took the baby with her.

Weeks later, Tim came home from work and found a letter on the kitchen table. It read: "Tim, come get your baby daughter." It gave him the name and address of where he could find his 15-month-old girl. Tim retrieved Sandy from the stranger's house and brought her home. A few days later Sandra begged for forgiveness and asked if she could return home. Tim let her return with a promise of making the effort to be a better mother—and a more loyal wife.

It wasn't long before Sandra returned to her old ways. This time Tim wasted no time and filed for divorce. He got sole custody of Sandy, something that Sandra never contested. Sandra was ordered to pay $35 a week in child support. She never made any payments, nor did she offer any excuses. Tim tried to collect from Sandra, but she never lived at one place long enough for him to get legal action in force. Sandra lived the life of a gypsy and never called to inquire about the welfare of her child.

Two years later Tim married a girl named Mary. Mary was the "love of his life." She also adored Sandy as much as she did her own young son from a failed marriage. They were, in Tim's words, "one big happy family." But tragedy interfered. Mary suffered a debilitating aneurysm of the brain.

Hospitalization and doctor bills put the family in deep debt, a debt that couldn't be satisfied by Tim's salary driving trucks. Mary had multiple seizures every day, all witnessed by 4-year-old Sandy. Tim thought it had a devastating effect on his little girl.

Personality changes were brought on by the insidious affliction, and it went on for two years. Mary subsequently was struck with two more aneurysms. Realistically looking at her prognosis and the chances of returning to a normal life, she decided that, since her medical bills were ruining the family finances, it would be best for Tim and her to divorce. It would give Tim and Sandy a chance to get on with their lives without the burdens of her disease. Mary moved in with her mother. At this writing Mary is a bedridden invalid.

Three years later, lonely and in need of a mother for his young child, Tim Ketchum got involved with another woman, Tracey. Sandy was not yet a teenager.

Tracey had a good steady job as a postal worker over in nearby Macon and a child from a previous marriage. In many ways she was a prize, what with a steady job and a willingness to take on the chores of motherhood. When Tim dated her, she fawned over Sandy, unable, it seemed, to give the little girl enough attention. Tim, looking back, could recognize that Tracey was "reeling him in." Tracey, according to him, was intent on snagging a husband.

The couple began to live together, buying a house and two brand-new cars. In December 1999 Tracey gave birth to Tim's second daughter. They named her Payton. The new family quickly experienced problems. Tim noticed that Tracey seemed to be "hollering all the time at Sandy." His sister Glenda noticed that Tracey's daughter and Payton were treated better. Her daughters got more gifts at Christmas. Sandy always seemed to be getting in trouble with her stepmother. She was constantly being disciplined. Tracey sent Sandy to her room for hours upon end. After a few incidents of Sandy slamming her bedroom door in frustration, Tracey removed the door.

Tim, a veteran of domestic problems, could see that it was having a bad effect on his young daughter. One of the manifestations of how it troubled her was that she didn't want to go to school in the morning and had to be forcibly taken there. The couple remained together for almost four years, even though things got "worse and worse" in Tim Ketchum's words. In time he suspected that Tracey was physically abusing Sandy. One afternoon he caught his wife in the act.

Arriving home early from work, he heard some horrible screaming coming from Sandy's room. Alarmed, he rushed into the room to find Tracey pinning Sandy to the bed with her knees, beating the child. Tim had to physically pull his wife off the pre-teen. According to Tim things cooled down after that ugly incident. But the peaceful interlude did not last long.

Tim received a call one day at work from a neighbor telling him that Tracey was "beating Sandy with her fists on her head." Tim raced home and confronted his wife. He didn't want to believe it, and Tracey denied it had ever happened, but a tearful Sandy confirmed it when her dad pulled her aside and asked her for the truth.

A few days later, 13-year-old Sandy ran off. After school she got on a different bus with a schoolmate and fled from the prospect of another day with her step-mother. Tim finally located the runaway after making some phone calls, and picked her up. When asked why she hadn't returned home after school, Sandy told her dad that she couldn't take the abuse anymore. He was devastated by this revelation. How could he have been so blind to Sandy's plight? Tim Ketchum resolved at that moment what he had to do next.

The following day Tim picked up his daughter after school and told her they were leaving. They went back to the Forsyth home they shared with Tracey, loaded up everything of theirs, and moved in with Tim's mother. Payton, Tim and Tracey's daughter, was left in the care of Tracey.

The couple was granted an uncontested divorce, and Tim was ordered to pay support for Payton. Shortly af-ter, Tim had to have surgery to correct a hernia problem that had kept him out of work for three months. As a result, he fell behind in his child support. Tracey refused Tim visitation rights and, since he could not afford a lawyer, had to sign an agreement drawn up by Tracey's lawyer that freed him of child support at the price of not being able to see Payton. It pained him deeply, but he had no other options. He was broke, out of work, and living at his mother's. All he had was Sandy. Sandy grieved over the separation from her half sister, and still does to this day.

Things began to look up for Tim when, one evening at the local VFW Hall, he met Beth. According to Tim the couple immediately "hit it off" and started dating.

Within a few weeks, Beth invited Tim and Sandy to move in with her in her little one-room apartment in Griffin. Beth had a good job, and Tim was on the mend both physically and emotionally. Within weeks the couple decided to move back to Fayetteville, the town Tim grew up in, so that they could enroll Sandy in the better school system. That done, Tim Ketchum was confident that he and Sandy, with Beth's help, had turned the corner. But, according to Tim, that was when "all hell broke loose."

At the Fayetteville Middle School, Sandy fell in with the wrong crowd. She and her friends began smoking marijuana, staying out late without permission, and cutting class. Beth would take her to school in the morning and drop her off at the front door, only to have Sandy immediately exit the back door. Amazingly Sandy got good grades in school, her stepmother Beth calling her "brain smart." She didn't study or do her homework, but she still managed to get all A's and B's.

Problems escalated from minor mischievous of-fenses to more serious ones, such as being caught in possession of diet pills. Her behavior at home was erratic, okay some days and moody and difficult on others, said Beth Ketchum.

Within a few months Sandy had been suspended from school three times because of drug use, so Tim and Beth put her in a rehabilitation center on her school's recommendation. Sandy promptly ran away. The rebellious teen was then remanded by the courts to a juvenile center in distant Macon. Tim and Beth made the long trip every weekend to visit their wayward daughter, at great expense of time and money. When Sandy was released, the couple decided it was time to leave Fayetteville and all the temptations Sandy would run up against once back home with her family.

The Ketchums never had a problem with Holly Harvey, Sandy's friend from the school. As far as they knew, she was a nice polite kid. Of all Sandy's friends, Holly was the one Tim and Beth liked best. The couple recalled how Holly would have her hair pulled up and bunched in a curly bun, wore tasteful make-up, cute shirts, and blue jeans. A "pretty little girl," they would agree.

Sandy dressed "different." She wore big baggy pants and shirts that made her parents conclude she was a tomboy. Tim tried to interest her in sports to no avail; all she wanted to do was hang out with her friends. Sandy did show an interest in boys, and it was not uncommon for some to visit, but her main interest was Holly Harvey.

She had come to their house on numerous occasions and spent many nights over, staying with Sandy in her room. Beth Ketchum often took Sandy to Holly's mom's house so they could spend the night together there. Beth always made a point of speaking with Carla Harvey to make sure it was all right.

When Carla went to jail, Holly was staying with Connie Earwood, and sometimes on weekends with her grandparents or her Uncle Kevin. Both Beth and Tim knew Kevin and thought highly of him. They had no qualms about leaving their girl in his care.

Tim and Beth didn't learn that Holly's grandparents disapproved of Sandy and didn't permit the girls to see each other until the two ran off to Sandy's natural mother Sandra's home in Griffin. The Ketchums didn't know that Sandy had initiated communications with Sandra, as she had done it on the sly.

Beth Ketchum met Carl and Sarah Collier for the first time at Kevin's house when everybody was looking for the missing pair in early June. Beth remembers the meeting as "cordial." When the girls were found at Sandra's house and returned home, Beth received a phone call from Sarah Collier.

Sarah said she did not think it was good for the girls to hang out together or speak with one another. Beth agreed and had already decided to forbid Sandy from contacting Holly. When Sandy got home, she was told of the ban. She asked if she could ever see Holly again, or was the ban "forever"? Beth never intended it to be and told Sandy so.

When Holly had run off again a week later, Sarah Collier called Beth Ketchum again, asking if they knew her whereabouts and if Sandy was with her. Sandy was standing right next to her stepmother at the time of the call and Beth told Sarah that. It was then that Sarah Collier asked if they knew the girls were gay and were involved romantically. Beth couldn't believe it. Sure, Holly stayed over, and the two slept in the same bed, but didn't all teenage girls do that? As a teenager, Beth had slept with her girlfriends, but they hadn't been gay. It had never crossed her mind that anything was going on sexually between the two girls. Beth remembered that Sandy had said that she "loved" Holly, but surely that was just innocent infatuation.

Beth asked Sarah Collier what possessed her to say such things. The elderly woman simply replied that Holly had told her so and that Holly was in love with Sandy. Not long after talking to Sarah Collier, the mother of one of Sandy's friends had called and asked if she knew that Sandy was gay. Beth investigated the claim on her own. While Sandy was at school she searched her stepdaughter's room. She found notes and poems to the girl whose mother had called, and to Holly Harvey. Beth confronted the teenager.

Sandy confessed to being bi-sexual. Beth was flabbergasted and didn't know how to respond when Sandy asked her if she knew what that meant. Beth, of course, knew what it meant, but didn't know how to say that to the 16-year-old in front of her. Beth cited Sandy's hormonal changes and the fact that she was still in the process of becoming "a little lady" and couldn't really know what she was at such a young age. Sandy countered that she was "all grown-up" and knew exactly what she was. Regardless, Beth told her, Sandy was her child and she still loved her no matter what her proclivity was. But she made it clear, in no uncertain terms, that her atypical sexual behavior would not be tolerated in her house. Sandy pressed her by asking what that meant. Holly, Beth replied, would not be permitted in their home and the girls would not be allowed to visit or speak with each other. According to Beth Ketchum, Sandy was "not too happy" with the ban.

Tim Ketchum was stunned at the revelation of his young daughter's sexual orientation. He was not pleased about it, but he was resolved to live with it, since, no matter what, he still loved his first-born. By early July the Ketchums had finally achieved some semblance of financial security, due to their hard work. They bought a house over in Franklin, in distant Heard County on the Alabama border, and made plans to move yet again. They took Sandy to see it, and she seemed pleased with the roomy house and wide-open spaces. But she had not shaken her infatuation with Holly Harvey.

When the Ketchums returned home with Sandy, the phone was ringing. Beth answered. Holly was on the other end of the line. She asked if she could speak with Sandy. Beth said no. Holly wanted to know why she couldn't speak with her girlfriend. Beth informed her that she would only be telling her this once: "Do not ever call my house again. This is my house, my phone, do not call here. You are not allowed to see Sandy, or talk to Sandy. Period! Do you understand?"

Holly's response was: "For how long?"

Beth told her: "Forever, it's over, it's done with."

That said, Beth slammed down the phone. At that moment Sandy walked into the room, having listened to the whole conversation from her room. "Why were you so mean to Holly?" she demanded to know. Beth denied that she was mean. She was being firm and she'd meant every word. She was tired of all the "crap." There would be no more Holly in Sandy's life, and she advised her stepdaughter to forget her.

Beth spent the next four days in the house alone with Sandy. She knew if she took her eyes off her, Sandy would clear out. Beth thought her relationship with Holly was a "phase thing" and that Sandy would get over her. The two kept their conversation to just small talk, and Beth pointedly kept away from any mention of Holly, hoping to avoid angry recriminations.

Sandy asked if she could talk to her biological mother. Tim and Beth, although not pleased with involving Sandra, reluctantly allowed Sandy to phone her. Sandy retreated to her room with the phone and dialed the Griffin number.

The next day, when Tim returned from work, Sandy told him that she wanted to have a "relationship" with her real mother. She thought that it was time to get to know her, and maybe develop a mother–daughter bond that she'd never had. Tim told Beth. Beth was hurt by the request, since she had been the only real mother Sandy had ever known. It was Beth who'd helped feed and clothe the girl and taken care of her the best she could. Sandra never gave a damn about the poor, mixed-up kid she'd given birth to so long ago. She never called Sandy. There were never any birthday cards or letters from her. She was, in effect, a perfect stranger to the 16-year-old girl whom she'd deserted almost fourteen years earlier.

Beth reminded Tim just "what kind of woman she was." Tim didn't have to be reminded. By this time Sandra had six children, all by different men, and had custody of none of them. Presently she was living in a run-down neighborhood in Griffin with another man of questionable character. Beth thought it was not a good idea for Sandy to move in with Sandra, and made it clear to both father and daughter.

Tim and Beth both tried to dissuade Sandy from seeing her birth mom, but she was adamant. Sandy brought up that Beth had never known her "birth daddy" until she was 18 years old. Beth couldn't argue that point.

The next day Tim conferred with Sandy's probation officer. The officer counseled that it might not be such a bad idea. Sandy was enduring some emotional tumult, and getting to know her birth mother might have a soothing effect on the troubled teen. Tim reluctantly agreed that Sandy could move in with her mother for "a while."

Beth Ketchum sat on her front porch as Sandy got her things ready. Beth was mad at Tim for letting her go and she was also mad at Sandy. Sandy came outside and asked her stepmother for a suitcase to pack her things in. Beth told her to find one herself, adding that she didn't approve of her moving in with Sandra and in no way would she be a part of it.

When Sandy was all packed, Beth walked into the room and noticed she had unplugged her TV set and stereo system and placed them alongside her packed bag. Beth asked what she was planning to do with those. Sandy replied she was taking them with her to her mom's. "No, no, no," Beth said. Anything she'd accumulated, things that Tim and Beth had bought for her while under their care, would stay there. Beth told Sandy that from now on, if there was anything she needed, she could ask her "mama." When Sandy came back to her real home, Beth told her, her stuff would be where she'd left it.

When it came time for Sandy to leave, Beth broke down in tears, and at the last moment climbed into the car with Tim and Sandy. Sandy was her child, she reasoned, and as her mother, Beth should see her off and see where she would be living. She knew that Sandy was not going into a good situation, and she was right.

Sandra was waiting for them. Beth immediately took her aside and told Sandra that Sandy was "her child" and looked to Beth as being her mother. She warned Sandra that she had "Sandy's life in her hands and that Sandra had better not let anything happen to Sandy." Beth told Sandra that Sandy was on probation and gave her the dates when Sandy had to meet with her probation officer. One part of the official stipulations was that Sandy was not to see Holly. Sandra would also have to enroll Sandy in the local school, and Beth gave her all of the medical records and school transcripts.

Sandra's home, in the words of Beth Ketchum, was "nasty." Walking in, they were greeted by two large dogs that had free rein in the house. There was a dog pen full of puppies that reeked of feces and urine in the living area. Two more large dogs barked incessantly from another pen in the backyard. Beth inspected the rest of the house, holding her breath so not as to smell the foul odor that permeated it. "Dog shit was everywhere."

The room Sandy put her belongings in was unpainted and cluttered with junk. Beth just about "puked" at the sight of it. Beth and Tim were hoping that Sandy would be repulsed by her accommodations. They begged her to reconsider the move, but she insisted she wanted to be with her natural mother. The disappointed couple could only hope that Sandy would come to her senses and call them to take her home from her vile surroundings.

Resigned to the fact that Sandy was adamant about staying with Sandra, a woman that she really didn't know, the Ketchums finally hugged and kissed Sandy and quietly left. They had done their best to convince their daughter her place was with them. The couple did not utter a word to each other on the hour's drive back home. Little did they know that leaving Sandy with Sandra would set in motion a chain of events that would culminate in the horrible and tragic day of August 2.

FIVE

Kevin Collier was supposed to drop his niece off at his parents' house on Monday, July 14, after she'd spent the weekend with him. His parents knew and had okayed the weekend stay-over with the Earwoods, but were unaware she had company—Sandy Ketchum. Kevin wasn't about to enlighten them. He knew, of course, of their disapproval of the friendship, but thought his strict parents were overreacting. Besides, Kevin found it difficult to say no to Holly.

Kevin and his father, Carl, worked together every weekday morning house-painting. Having retired from Delta, Carl kept himself active and supplemented his pension with the thriving business. The father-and-son team were, as Kevin recalled, always busy, and there was a backlog of jobs to be done. Even at the age of 74, his dad showed no signs of slowing down. Carl Collier handled the workload as well as any man half his age. Kevin worked with his dad from 8 AM to 12 PM and then went home to get ready for his job at Delta.

Kevin returned home at around 12:30 PM. After getting ready for work, he would drive Holly back up to his parents' house on his way to the airport. Back at his house he found Holly and Sandy gone. Kevin could already hear the blistering admonishment from his mom for permitting the two girls to stay at his house again.

Kevin got both barrels. As soon as she got off the phone with her son, Sarah Collier filed a child runaway complaint with the sheriff's department and then drove down to the house in Griffin where she knew she would find her granddaughter. She was right.

On Monday, July 26, 2004, Holly was accompanied by her grandparents to the Fayette County Courthouse, where she was ordered to appear in front of the juvenile court for running away. The court, after hearing the case, required Holly to submit to random drug testing and "not to associate with anyone under court supervision [i.e. Sandy]." She also had to attend a three-week program called Breaking the Chain. The course was created "to help troubled teens learn to make better choices for a better future." Holly also got three months' probation and was released to her grandparents' custody. After being excused by the court, the 15-year-old stormed outside. Once in the bright July sun, Holly lit a cigarette. It was one of the few vices Holly ascribed to that was tolerated by her grandparents. Holly and the Colliers walked to Carl's late model Chevy truck in silence. The Colliers could see that Holly was incensed by the humiliation of the court appearance and sentence. Holly strode up to the truck as her grandparents got in, took one last drag of her cigarette, and crushed it out on the hood of her granddad's pride and joy. It was an act of defiance and disrespect that made the normally patient and understanding Carl explode. He grabbed Holly by the arm and hollered while shaking his granddaughter that he was brining her right back to court. They could keep her for all he cared.

Sarah intervened. "No, no, no," she pleaded, calming Carl down. Holly had been through enough that morning, she cried, saying, "Let's just go home."

Holly turned to her grandparents with a snarl and said, "I'm gonna kill y'all."

Carl Collier said nothing about the incident to his son the next day. They were so busy working that Kevin forgot to ask about Holly's court appearance. On Wednesday morning the subject finally came up. His father told him about her hearing and the ugly incident with the cigarette. He also told his son that Holly had threatened to kill them. Kevin advised his dad that if he saw any little thing out of the ordinary he should call 911. But Kevin knew that his parents would never involve the police, since they knew Holly would pull some of Carla's old tricks, such as banging her head against the wall or causing some other self-injury, and blame it on her grandparents. The Colliers didn't want any trouble with the police. Kevin wasn't too worried, since he thought Holly was just being a disrespectful "smartass" and the 15-year-old was hardly capable of overpowering her much bigger and stronger granddad.

Kevin thought a lot about the situation over the next

few days. He couldn't help but think that Holly was just like a caged animal in the house on Plantation Drive. When she was with her mom there were no rules and she could do whatever she damned well felt like. She could smoke inside, drink beer, and smoke dope. At her grandparents', there was none of that. The wild teenager was being domesticated against her will. Kevin knew it must have driven his niece crazy, but Holly was also "sneaky." When her grandparents were upstairs, she was downstairs. When they were downstairs, she was outside. But his parents weren't stupid. They knew what she was up to, and that she snuck out of the house whenever she could.

From jail Carla wrote her daughter a letter commiserating about what a "messed up" deal she'd gotten being put on probation. Carla warned her that if she cared about her freedom, she had "better fly right and straighten up."

Carla also inquired about the "living conditions" at her parents' home, and how she couldn't stand the thought of Holly being there and what she "had to go through."

After requesting some of her jewelry and some make-up, Carla ended the letter by saying how sorry she was for what she'd put Holly through, but how happy they would be once they were together again. Carla advised her "to just hang in there," since it would "be all over soon."

Carla enclosed a cartoon she had cut out of a magazine. It graphically illustrated her jailhouse wisdom. It portrayed two fish eyeing a baited hook. One of them advised the other, "Keep your mouth shut, and you won't get caught."

On July 31, Holly got another letter, this time from Sandy. Sandy vented about what was bothering her. Holly had accused her of still being infatuated with another love interest and of planning to dump Holly for her. In the letter Sandy assured her lover that she didn't love Amanda anymore, writing that "it was in the past." She implored Holly to realize what she had done to be with her. She plaintively asked why they couldn't forget the past and "live in the present." She further wrote:

> *I love you so fuckin' much that it drives [me] crazy not to be with U everyday! I mean damn! What do I have to do???*

Sandy explained that it was 4:40 AM and everything was in "slow motion" since she had been taking drugs and drinking.

Sandy cryptically ended her letter by writing the following:

> *We're on fire! Anyways . . . damn! Can I put it in your mouf? Or can you put it in my mouf? Let me kno [sic] nigga! LOL! Damn! Sara's pregnant, Amanda's pregnant, who's next? Not you I hope! LOL! Well, I glad 'cause I'm so fuckin' not. Blaze one.*
>
> *Love ya,*
Sandy.

Sandy attached a poem she penned:

> *I try so hard,*
> *To really let you know,*
> *How much I love you,*
> *But it's a price to pay though!*
>
> *You don't understand,*
> *That I've let go of the past.*
> *That I want to be with you,*
> *And I want it to last.*
>
> *You just can't believe,*
> *That you're the one for me.*
> *And that in your arms,*
> *Is where I want to be.*
>
> *I wake up in the morning,*
> *And I ask myself.*
> *Is life worth living?*
> *Or should I just blast myself?*
>
> *Then I think of you,*
> *And know my life is worth living,*
> *But what would I do,*
> *If our love had no meaning.*

Sandy Ketchum. . . . To be continued. . . .

On Sunday, August 1, Brittany Anne Jensen received a call from Holly at about 8:45 PM. Brittany couldn't pick up the phone, but listened to the message on her answering machine. Holly sounded "a little upset," so Brittany called her right back. She apologized for not calling her in a while, but said she would love to see her. The problem was that she and Holly didn't drive and had nobody to help them get Holly to Brittany's home in Lithia Springs.

At 9:00 PM Brittany said she had to get off the phone, but promised to call back soon. Holly blurted out that she hated her grandparents, especially her grandma, and how she didn't respect them. Living with them was hell. Brittany commiserated with her for a few moments, and then said goodbye.

On the morning of Monday, August 2, as per usual, Kevin worked with his dad painting a house in Fayetteville. At noon he cleaned up, bade his father goodbye, and headed to work at the airport. Nothing, Kevin remembered, was out of the ordinary on the hot summer day other than his having to leave work early to attend orchestra practice at First Baptist Church in Dunwoody.

At about 3:00 PM Chris Miller, a family friend, called Sarah Collier about some books she had loaned him. They agreed that he would give them to Carl later that evening when he saw him at their local church meeting in Jonesboro. Sarah told Miller that she was planning a vacation to Hawaii and was leaving the following Monday. She sounded exhausted and mentioned that Carl had urged her to go, since she needed "to get away." Sarah had been reluctant to go and leave Carl with the job of looking after Holly, who Miller knew was a problem child. Miller asked if Carla was getting out of jail soon and she told him that she assumed it would be in another month. Sarah said it "would be great" to have Carla assume the parental duties again. She admitted that Holly was "killing us," that she slept all day, smoked pot, and would sneak out of the house at night. She went on to relate that their son, Kevin, would help Carl look after Holly while she was gone, and how her son was much better equipped to handle the 15-year-old.

Miller told Sarah how he wished they would try getting Holly in the Georgia Baptist Children's Home. Sarah said they had no authority to do so, since they were not the legal guardians. Miller ended the call by wishing her well on her vacation and to be sure to call when she returned home. He told Sarah he loved her and she replied by saying she loved him too, and hung up the phone.

Carl Collier never made it to the church meeting.

At 3:30 PM Holly called her friend Amanda Roberts. She pleaded with Amanda to come pick up her and Sandy at 226 Plantation Drive, telling her that they needed "to get away." Amanda told her schoolmate that she couldn't, since she didn't know how to drive. Holly abruptly hung up the phone.

At 4:37 PM Samantha Colon received a call from Sandy Ketchum. Sandy asked her if she knew where to get a gun. Samantha told Sandy no and asked why she needed one. Sandy's reply was "So I can take care of business." Samantha then turned to her boyfriend, Marc Aragon, and sarcastically asked him if he knew where to get a gun. Marc took the phone and spoke with Sandy. Sandy asked Marc at least "six or seven times" where she could get a gun. Marc kept asking her why she needed one so badly. Sandy wouldn't answer. Frustrated at the non-response, he handed the phone back to Samantha.

The shaky voice on the phone admitted to Samantha that she "was scared." When Samantha pressed her for a reason, Sandy said, "I just am, I'm gonna go to jail for murder." Samantha pleaded with her friend not to do anything stupid, and told her to come to Fayetteville sometime soon to see her. Sandy said goodbye and the line went dead.

Sarah Collier had a great sense of smell, and in the early evening hours of August 2, she noticed a strange aroma emanating from the basement of the house. Holly had been locked in her finished basement room, her mother Carla's old room, all day, loud rock music blaring from behind the closed door.

When Carl got home from work, Sarah told him she thought she smelled the pungent scent of marijuana coming from Holly's room. Sarah had reservations for a flight to Hawaii the following Monday to visit an old friend. With the excuse of gathering some luggage that was stored in Holly's closet, the couple descended the stairs from the kitchen. Carl tried the door, but it was locked. He knocked and asked Holly to unlock it so they could retrieve the luggage. Sarah followed her husband into the room when the lock clicked open.

As Carl rummaged through the closet, his wife screamed. Turning around, he could tell that Sarah was bleeding and saw Holly standing there with a boning knife in her hand. He lunged for his granddaughter. Carl, aided by his wounded wife, quickly pinned Holly to the bed and grabbed for the knife. Holly hollered, imploring "Aren't you gonna help me?" The Colliers didn't know who Holly was screaming for, and were surprised when Sandy Ketchum jumped out from behind Holly's bed. The four-person melee commenced.

Severely slashed and bleeding profusely, Carl broke away and ran for the phone that sat on a table in the living area between the two downstairs bedrooms. Holly chased after him. Blood from Carl's wounds sprayed the hallway walls. Before Carl could dial 911, Holly cut the phone line with the knife and proceeded to whale away on her grandfather with it. Carl managed to escape the frenzied attack and lurched up the stairs with Holly in pursuit.

In the meantime Sandy continued the murderous attack on Sarah in the basement. Sarah had managed to stumble out of the bedroom, but only got to the foot of the stairs, where she collapsed. Convinced that Sarah Collier was no longer an impediment, Sandy stood over the body and watched as life blood gushed from the numerous knife wounds.

Even though severely wounded, Carl tried to fend off Holly. In the kitchen he grabbed for the wall-mounted phone. With the receiver in one hand, he fought off the girls' attack with the other. Holly tore the phone off the wall. Trying to avoid the flailing knife, Carl staggered around the kitchen island, leaving a trail of blood. Holly was relentless, frantically stabbing him a total of twenty-seven times. He finally succumbed to the ferocious onslaught and collapsed on the kitchen floor.

At approximately 5 PM Amanda Roberts got another phone call from Holly. This time Holly told her that she and Sandy needed to find some drugs, and asked for a dealer friend's number. Amanda claimed she didn't know it. She could hear Sandy in the background frantically talking with Holly. Holly replied by saying it was an emergency and then abruptly hung up.

At 7:25 PM Samantha Colon picked up her ringing phone. Holly was on the line. Holly told her to be sure to watch the 10 o'clock news on TV and that she would be "surprised" at what she would see.

At 7:26 PM Holly made another phone call from her grandmother's cell phone. This time it was to another friend, Virginia Roberts. Holly told her to watch the evening news. When Virginia asked why, Holly hung up.

SIX

Sara Polk, 15 years of age, had known Sandy Ketchum since they were both 11. They had met when Sara lived with her grandmother in Fayetteville and they were both attending the same primary school. Sara thought that Sandy was "pretty cool," and they became best friends and "hung out together all the time." When her parents got a place of their own in Griffin and moved to neighboring Spalding County, the two girls still kept in touch, but did not see each other quite as often as before. The teenagers hooked up when Sandy visited family in Griffin or when Sara was in Fayetteville, but they had grown apart.

Three years had passed when the two re-established a tight friendship. In the interim the two had not been able to see each other because Sandy was on probation as a result of drug and fighting infractions at school. Sara Polk somehow had appeared on Sandy's probation officer's list of problem friends, although she denied ever being into drugs herself. Sandy's parents, informed of the ban, made sure it was enforced.

When Sandy and Sara finally saw each other again it was the summer of 2004, when Sandy moved in with her mother Sandra in Griffin. Sara didn't think Sandra Ketchum was a "nice person," and was even worse as a mother. Her house was a pig sty and she left Sandy to her own devices, including hitchhiking to wherever she had to go.

Sara Polk was shocked at what Sandy had become. She was in trouble in school and in constant battles with her father and stepmother. Sara advised her long-time friend that she had to "straighten out."

It was at Sandra's house where Sara Polk first met Holly Harvey. Sara, who had just gotten back from a funeral, made a surprise visit to Sandy's mom's house. Holly was hanging out after running away from home to be with Sandy. Sandy was clearly embarrassed that Holly was there. Sara took an immediate disliking to her when Holly noticeably became jealous of the attention Sandy was showering on Sara. After an uncomfortable hour, Sandy finally persuaded Holly to arrange for her grandmother to pick her up at the Wal-Mart in Griffin. The long-time teenage friends waited with Holly until Sarah Collier arrived.

Sara had known that Sandy was a lesbian from the time they were 11 years old, though she liked guys too—"just anybody warm" as Sara would later explain. Sandy loved Holly, Sara knew that. It was because Holly paid attention to her and showered affection on the awkward 15-year old tomboy. And Holly was pretty. Sandy didn't like her own looks. She was self-conscious about the eczema she suffered from, which had her always wearing long-sleeve shirts and long pants, even in the warm Georgia summers. According to the perky and cute Sara, "guys never chased after Sandy."

The reason for Sandy moving into her mother's house was pretty clear to Sarah Polk. Sandra let Sandy do anything she wanted, and that included having Holly over or letting her barely pubescent daughter thumb a ride up to Riverdale to see her at her grandparents'. Neither Sandy's parents, nor Holly's grandparents would ever have permitted that.

Sandy had always had a thing for Sara. She would call her and write letters and poems to her expressing her love. But Sara had always been "boy-crazy" and Sandy hated that. Sara loved her as a friend and wanted only the best for her, but she couldn't be "with her like Sandy wanted."

Sara also knew the two were into drugs, doing them "24/7," but Sandy had done drugs for a long time anyway, so Sara couldn't lay that blame on Holly. Sandy was partial to "chronic," a street name for marijuana laced with cocaine. She also smoked "wet," which was marijuana or tobacco dipped in embalming fluid, formaldehyde, or PCP. Also known on the street as "sherm" or "fry," the heinous concoction is extremely hallucinogenic, causing users to feel like everything is moving fast as their bodies seem to heat up. When "full-blasted," bizarre, paranoid, and violent behavior is a common reaction to the drug. A two-ounce vial of "wet" goes for about $50 on the street.

Sara continued to see and hear from Sandy on a regular basis, since she was now living in Griffin with her mother, but Sara knew Sandy was spending a lot of time in Fayetteville seeing Holly.

On the night of August 1 Sara got a phone call from Sandy. She was with Holly. Sandy just wanted "to chill and talk" but Sara had her first day in eleventh grade the next morning and just wanted to go to bed, so she kept the conversation short. Sara had trouble sleeping that night. Her chest and back were bothering her, and she just knew something bad was going to happen. Her gut feeling said it would somehow involve her childhood friend Sandy Ketchum.

The next day, in the early evening hours, Sara got another phone call from Sandy. She knew it was coming from Holly's grandmother's cell phone from the caller ID. Holly and Sandy were coming to Sara's house in Griffin because they were "covered in blood" since they "got jumped" and needed a place to clean up. The rest of the call was all "gibberish," according to Sara.

Sara's sister was in town from Indiana and Sara didn't want her to "freak out" at seeing the troublesome pair, especially if they were covered in blood from being mugged. Sara told them not to come. Holly and Sandy showed up anyway, at about 6:00 PM, minutes after the phone call. Holly was behind the wheel of a large blue Chevrolet pickup truck. Sara was on the phone with her boyfriend. She went out to meet them, still on the wireless phone with her beau. She didn't want the pair coming into the house. Holly and Sandy were drenched in blood and "stunk." The stench had the distinct smell of iron, blood, Sara surmised. The two girls pleaded with Sara that they needed help, since they had been attacked and needed to clean up. Sara studied them and noted that they didn't seem to be injured. Both Sandy and Holly were nervously puffing away on Newport cigarettes. Finally Holly blurted out that they had just killed her grandparents. Holly seemed excited about it, but Sandy was "white as a ghost."

Sara incredulously asked, "You killed your grandparents!" With the wireless phone still to her ear, she heard her boyfriend say "What?" and he immediately hung up the phone. Sara placed the phone down on the dashboard of the truck. She remembers asking the two, "Why, why, why?" Sandy, in a stupor, said she didn't know why, but admitted they were "all cracked out." Holly didn't have an answer.

Sandy begged Sara to let them in the house so they could take showers. Sara refused. She told Sandy that if she hadn't been covered in blood, she'd drag her out of the truck and "kick her ass." Sara's younger sister emerged from the house, but Sara waved her back in. Sara managed to maintain some semblance of sanity, thinking she had to get them away from her house, protect her family, and make sure she could not be connected to their crimes. She also wanted to know if Holly's grandparents were just injured or indeed dead. Maybe they were in need of help, she conjectured.

Sara returned to her house and grabbed a towel and soaked it in the kitchen sink. Tossing it to Sandy, she watched as the girls stripped naked on the dirt driveway. Sara was shocked to see that there was even blood on their underwear and socks. The girls hurriedly cleaned up with the white bath towel as Sara watched from her front door stoop. Sara then realized she had left her wireless phone on the truck's dashboard. She ran back down the driveway to the truck. Reaching for the phone, she saw a bloody kitchen butcher knife lying on the front cab floor. Thinking quickly, she told the two naked girls to dump their clothes and the murder weapons in the Flint River. Sara figured if she knew where they would dispose of the incriminating evidence, she could later tell the police. She just wanted them and any evidence to be as far from her and her home as possible.

Holly and Sandy hurriedly changed into clean clothes and tossed the bloodied ones in the rear cab of the truck. Without uttering another word, the pair climbed into the truck and sped off into the twilight.

Sara's parents arrived just as Holly and Sandy were leaving. Sara blurted out the story to her stunned mother, Jamie, who immediately dialed 911. Deputy D. W. Gibson of the Spalding County Sheriff's Office arrived minutes later at 6:20 PM. Sara told the officer everything she knew and showed them a snapshot of Sandy Ketchum. Gibson then had the 15-year-old write out a one-page statement.

To verify the outrageous claims of the fleeing fugitives, deputies had to find out the identity of the purported victims. They asked Sara to try to reach the girls on their cell phone. With the okay of the officers Sara retreated to her bedroom and punched in *69, which automatically redialed her last incoming call. It dialed Sarah Collier's cell phone.

The call was not picked up. Sara tried it again.

Sandy finally answered. Sara asked her long-time friend the names of Holly's grandparents—because reports were "all over the news" about a double homicide in the county. She was bluffing, since no news of the murders had been aired yet. Sara said she wanted to know if they were the grandparents of Holly Harvey. "Sara and Carl Collier" came the answer over the phone. She added that they lived on Plantation Drive in Riverdale up in Fayette County.

Sara told Sandy "they had better get out of town" quickly, asking where they would be heading. The line went dead. Sara realized that Sandy was "on to what I was doing." Sara tried re-dialing the number several times. The calls were never picked up.

Sara emerged from her room and gave the information to the deputy, who immediately called it in. Then they waited.

Sara didn't feel much like cooperating anymore. Sandy was her friend. Sara didn't feel she was wrong in giving her up to the cops, but she didn't want her to be caught—at least not yet. If she'd killed those people, Sara, in her teenage logic, thought she deserved to be apprehended, but should have time to think about what she had done before they threw the cuffs on her. Sara also had a hard time believing Sandy could actually kill anyone. She wouldn't put it past Holly, but Sandy? She had seemed so scared and confused. Holly had to be behind it all. Sandy just didn't have it in her. Sandy, Sara felt, never had a chance to be "just a kid."

Later that evening Sara was brought over to Griffin's Spalding County Sheriff's Office. Fayette County Sheriff's detectives Bo Turner and Phil McElwaney arrived shortly thereafter. After questioning the girl and having her attempt to call her fugitive friends, the detectives brought her home and had her call from there in an effort to determine where they were. Before the calls were made, unmarked police cars were placed strategically around the Polks' neighborhood in case the girls were still in the area. From previous calls made by Holly to Sara Polk, the police knew Holly was using her grandparents' stolen cell phone when they had fled the Plantation Drive house. By this time the US Marshals' Southeast Regional Fugitive Task Force (SERFTF) was involved.

When it was formed in 1983 SERFTF's sole purpose was to track down and arrest people for whom felony warrants had been issued. The task force was popularized in the motion picture *The Fugitive* with Tommy Lee Jones and Harrison Ford. The Fayette County Sheriff's Office has an attached member to their regional task force and this special deputy is empowered by the authority of the US Marshals to travel anywhere in the United States to track down and apprehend wanted fugitives from Fayette County.

It was an open secret that the service had the ways and means of tracking fugitives via any cell phone call, and the technology had vastly improved the system. As of this writing, there are two different systems used depending on what kind of cell service is being tracked. The capability is called E-911 and the programs used by the US Marshals are called *Triggerfish* and *Stingray*. In the last few years cell phones have been equipped with a Global Positioning System (GPS) chip, whereas the signal from a cell phone can be located anywhere in the world. The Marshal Service has the capability of locating the phone to within a few feet, even when it is not turned on. SERFTF knew the girls were heading in a southeasterly direction.

When Tim and Beth Ketchum returned home from work on August 2, their answering machine was blinking. The message had come from Tim's estranged sister Glenda, who asked for Tim to call. A man across the street from Glenda had been monitoring the police band radio. He'd walked across the street to ask her if the Sandy Ketchum the police were looking for in connection with a double homicide in Riverdale was the daughter of her brother.

Beth immediately dialed Glenda's number. Glenda answered and refused to talk to her, telling her to put her brother on the line. Tim took the phone. Seconds later Tim slowly hung up the phone, sat on the couch, buried his face in his hands, and cried uncontrollably. Beth couldn't get a word out of him. She quickly redialed Glenda's number and demanded to know what she had said to Tim that had him on the verge of collapse.

Glenda again refused to talk to her sister-in-law, telling her to "ask Tim." Beth informed her that Tim was unable to tell her because of his hysterical condition. She wanted to hear it from Glenda. The terse reply was swift in coming: "Sandy has gone an' killed some-damn-body. Is that good enough for yer?" The line went dead. Before Beth could replace the phone receiver to its cradle, the top news story for the local 11 o'clock news had come on. It was a report of the murders of the elderly couple in Riverdale—Carl and Sarah Collier.

The phone calls began to pour in. Word had spread fast. The Ketchums got in their car and sped down to Sandra's house in Griffin. At first Sandra "played dumb," saying she had no idea where Sandy was, but then the man she was living with emerged from a bedroom and proceeded to "cuss her out" screaming that she knew damn well where Sandy had gone. Flustered, Sandra finally confessed that her neighbor had driven Sandy to Holly's grandparents' house in Riverdale the day before. That was all Tim and Beth needed to know to confirm their worst fears. Sandy was somehow involved in the murders of the Colliers.

Heartbroken, the Ketchums drove over to a friend's house in Griffin. The Spalding County sheriff's deputies arrived and requested that they all remain at the house in case the girls returned to seek refuge with family.

Sara Polk, with the detectives hovering around her, called the number several times over the course of an hour and a half. She got the voice mail for the number each time. Coming to the conclusion that Holly and Sandy wouldn't be answering or calling back anytime soon, Turner and McElwaney returned to their offices at the Fayette County Sheriff's Office, where they found their superior Bruce Jordan delegating tasks to his men.

Turner had only worked on an occasional case with Jordan, but was still in awe of the man. This evening he was getting an up-close and personal look at how the vaunted lawman worked. Turner found he was having trouble keeping up with the rapid tangential thought processes of his commander. It took both Turner and McElwaney to get written down in their notebooks all the things Jordan wanted done. Detective Ethon Harper was given the task of securing arrest warrants for Holly Harvey and Sandy Ketchum from a magistrate judge.

An all points bulletin was put out on the missing truck that belonged to Carl Collier. Bo Turner remembers that there were dozens of things going on, and then, at about 12 midnight, Jordan had everyone stop what they were doing and sit down around the sheriff's office conference table. He set down a stack of color photographs removed from the Collier house, looked at his men, and asked, "Where do you think they're going to go?" All the gathered policemen offered their thoughts. Finally Jordan began to select photos from the stack and threw them on the table for his men to see. Every one of them was a picture of Holly at the seashore. All the assembled policemen were then polled again for their hunches. All came to the same conclusion: Holly was fleeing to the beach.

One of the first things Jordan had to find out was how they would charge the fugitive girls once they were apprehended. Jordan placed a call to District Attorney Bill McBroom. McBroom had decided to charge the girls as adults, and told Jordan he would have his staff research the legalities regarding the girls' Miranda rights and have it ready ASAP.

The DA's staff had all the research done. Assistant District Attorney Dan Hiatt had worked late into the evening. He provided Detective Harper with the legal ammunition he needed. Just before midnight Chief Magistrate Charles Floyd issued warrants for the arrest of Holly Harvey and Sandy Ketchum.

After obtaining the warrants Harper advised Young's Cleaning Service to transport the Colliers' bodies to the Georgia Bureau of Investigation's medical examiner's office in Atlanta.

At 1:15 AM the US Marshals' Fugitive Task Force notified Bruce Jordan at the Fayette County Sheriff's Office that Holly and Sandy were near Pooler, Georgia, on or near I-16. They appeared to be driving in a southeasterly direction.

Jordan asked for volunteers to fly down to ever-popular Daytona Beach, Florida, that night. Turner and McElwaney raised their hands. They felt they were the ones most qualified to go, since they had caught up with Holly after she had run away from her grandparents' home.

Jordan took the two detectives into his office, got on the Internet, found two open seats on a flight to Jacksonville, Florida, at 4:58 AM that morning, and booked them. From a safe he removed cash and a county credit card, and handed them over to Turner, then told them to have a safe flight.

Turner and McElwaney stopped at their respective homes on the way to the airport for a quick shower and a sandwich to go, and to pick up some spare clothes for a trip whose duration was anyone's guess. Arriving at the Atlanta airport, the two detectives presented letters from the sheriff's department allowing them to carry their handguns on the airplane. The pair arrived in

Jacksonville at 5:55 AM and from there went right to a rent-a-car place. There was a hang-up. Instructed to rent an economy car, the pair found that there were only full-size vehicles available. After some unsuccessful haggling with the rent-a-car agents, Turner called his boss back in Fayetteville. The exasperated Jordan told him he didn't care what kind of a car they rented, just as long as it got them to Daytona. Finally heading south to Daytona in the luxury car, Turner and McElwaney talked about searching all the cheap motel parking lots along the famous A1A Strip.

Early the next morning Detective Harper met with Tim and Beth Ketchum and relatives Mr. and Mrs. Larry Harmon in the sheriff's Public Information Office. Lieutenant Belinda McCastle, who headed that office, was in attendance. The family expressed the desire to issue a plea to Sandy to turn herself in. They provided more information on her, including distinguishing tattoos and her behavioral problems.

Beth Ketchum also told the police officers that she had found "kitchen-style knives" hidden in Sandy's bedroom several times in the past when she had gone in to discipline her. The family also told them that Sandra, Sandy's biological mother, had told them her neighbor gave Sandy a ride to the Colliers' home on Sunday, the day before the murders.

At approximately 9:00 AM on Tuesday, Bruce Jordan informed his team that the US Marshals' Fugitive Task Force had located the whereabouts of Holly Harvey and Sandy Ketchum. The E-911 tracking system had pinpointed their position on Tybee Island, Georgia. US Marshals dispatched from the Savannah office to Tybee had quickly located the blue Chevrolet Silverado parked in a beachfront lot.

Jordan was on the phone within minutes dialing Detective Bo Turner's cell phone. He told Turner that he and Detective Phil McElwaney should turn around and head directly to Savannah, Georgia, eighty-nine miles north of where they were. The two detectives acknowledged the directive and turned around. The trip would take just fifty minutes.

Jordan then ordered Chief Pilot Bill Riley to ready the department's helicopter for flight. Jordan had the head pilot steer a course for Tybee Island, some two hours distance by air. Two and a half hours later, the sheriff's department's helicopter landed near the lighthouse on Tybee Island.

SEVEN

Tybee Island has a long colorful history and a richly deserved reputation as a hip beach community. Along its coast, warm blue waters are greeted by sparkling white sands. Tybee, according to historians, derives its name from the Native American Euchee Indian word for "salt." The Spaniard Lucas Vásquez de Ayllón first explored the island in 1520 when he took possession of it for the Spanish Crown.

The encroaching French were first drawn to Tybee by reports of an abundance of the coveted sassafras roots. Sassafras was believed by Europeans of the day to be a cure-all for a variety of maladies.

The island's remoteness and the presence of fresh water drew many an infamous pirate to her shores throughout the sixteenth and seventeenth Centuries. Local legends have it that the island was a favorite stashing place for buccaneers intent on secreting away looted treasures.

Spain finally relinquished Tybee along with most of her territories along the eastern seaboard to the superior French and English forces that had arrived in the New World. In 1733 Tybee became key to the establishment of the new colony named after England's King George by General James Oglethorpe, who ordered a lighthouse and fort to be built on the island to protect the thriving port from marauding Spaniards and pirates. The island's strategic importance carried over into the War of 1812. American forces used the island's lighthouse as a signal tower to warn of a possible attack by the British.

In the Civil War the island was first held by the Confederate Army, but they were later forced to withdraw after ordered by General Robert E. Lee to defend the city of Savannah from the intimidating ramparts of Fort Pulaski. Union General Quincy Adams Gilmore took the island and immediately fortified it with the latest technologically advanced heavy gun batteries on the west side directly facing Fort Pulaski, which was less than a mile away. The cannon batteries fired the first-ever rifled shot at Fort Pulaski on April 11, 1862, and thus forever changed military strategy, making the brick and mortar fortresses obsolete due to their inability to withstand the awesome power of the new artillery.

In the 1870s residents of Savannah began to trickle onto the island to escape the sweltering heat of the coastal Georgia summers. By the 1890s the collection of beach houses had swelled to over 400 in number.

Throughout the past century the island's population had gradually shifted from summer to full-time residents, and now stands at 3,392, even though the tides have been eroding the island since such recordings were made in 1925. The FBI reported that in the 2003 calendar year there were just five violent crimes and no homicides committed on the island. Such a blissful setting drew throngs of sun worshippers, including well-known resident actress Sandra Bullock, to the shrinking sands of the island beaches. This was the world that the Clayton brothers and their mother thought they had set foot on on a sunny, pleasant day on August 3, 2004.

Brett Shremshock, 15, and brother Brian Clayton, 22, had arrived on Tybee Island early in the morning. Along with their mother, Patricia Pelleiren, they had spent the day unpacking and getting the house ready to be lived in. At about 8:00 PM Patricia left for work at a local hospital in Savannah, where she was a registered nurse. The movers and her kids continued hauling in boxes and furniture. When the movers finally finished at around 9:30 PM the boys decided they needed a break and went to check out their new surroundings.

They wandered a few blocks down to the North Beach area of the island. At about 10 PM they noticed two girls drive by in a blue truck. The truck stopped, turned around, and drove up to them. The two young brown-haired girls asked them for a cigarette. Brian thought they were kind of young to be in possession of the truck, a late model Silverado that was obviously well-maintained. Must belong to one of their dads, he thought. The girls asked what they were up to and Brian told them that he and his brother were going for a walk along the beach. The driver and the prettier of the two girls asked if they could join them, since they were new to the island and didn't know their way around. Brian hesitated and looked at his younger brother quizzically before saying, "I guess." The boys waited as the girls parked the truck and then proceeded to walk alongside Brian and Brett.

Brett remembers that the girls were "real quiet," so his brother tried to draw them into conversation. They appeared reluctant to talk.

Breaking the uncomfortable silence, Brett and Brian told the girls they had just moved to the island from the town of Winder in Barrow County, which lay between Athens and Atlanta. The reason, they said, was that their mother had tired of the crime problems in their old neighborhood. She didn't want to raise her boys in such an atmosphere. The girls nodded their understanding.

When asked what their names were, the girls looked at each other before the pretty one said "Casey and Krystal." Brian got the feeling that they were lying. While strolling along the beach the girls lit up a joint.

Holly asked the older boy if he could help them "get rid of the truck." Brian reminded the two that they too were new to the island and had no idea how they could do that. Then "Casey" showed them some gold jewelry that they wanted to pawn. She said it had belonged to her grandmother, who had recently died.

Back at the parked truck the girl who'd identified herself as Casey asked Brian if they could stay at their place for the night, since they had no money or a place to stay. Brian gave Brett another puzzled look. The unasked question was clear to the younger boy: "It was kinda weird that someone would come to a beach resort with no money or a place to crash," Brett remembered thinking. Brian finally said, "Yeah, I guess, but only for the night."

Casey and Krystal were clearly lesbians. Brian was struck by the way the two acted like "boyfriend and girlfriend" in their interactions. The body language and the way they touched each other sent out clear signals to Brian and Brett. Krystal also looked real "butchy."

The girls, when pressed on why they were on Tybee, said that they had just "needed to get away." It was on a whim that they had come to the island. They had hoped to hook up with some friends who lived here, who turned out not to be home. They confessed that they were hard-pressed about what to do. Suspicious of the two strange girls, Brian was looking for an out. He said their house was a mess because of the move, and that maybe the boys should ask their mom first if it was okay for Casey and Krystal to stay.

Brian detected an almost palpable unease from the girls. When he asked if anything was wrong, Casey said they "had a lot on their mind." Krystal simply nodded in agreement.

Before calling his mom, Brian offered the girls space in his first-floor bedroom over the open carport area of the beach house. He pulled the top mattress off his bed and the girls collapsed on it and quickly cuddled up in each other's arms.

From the kitchen Brian called his mother at work and asked if the two stray teenagers could stay. Patricia's answer was a quick "Hell no!" She told her son they had just moved in, the house was a mess, and they didn't know these kids. But by this time, Brian couldn't force himself to evict the two. They were comatose on the mattress.

Patricia arose around 10 the next morning after a

well-deserved sleep and was surprised to see the two teen girls emerge from Brian's room. She pulled her older son aside and asked what they were doing there, since she had unequivocally told him that they couldn't stay the night. Brian told her he was at a loss at what to do, since they had quickly fallen asleep in his room. He apologized to his resigned mother. She nodded her understanding of his predicament. Patricia shrugged her shoulders and said no more.

Brian and Brett both told their mother that they had gotten "bad vibes" from the girls and that "something was not right" about the pair. The boys couldn't help but notice how Casey and Krystal were always whispering to each other, and how one was "abnormally quiet." Brian told his mom that the girls made him "nervous" and they were obviously "up to something." He also related that the girls had said they had "taken a relative's truck." It didn't occur to him that they had actually stolen it.

Casey finally approached Patricia and the first words out of her mouth were whether she knew where a pawn shop was. "Good gracious, no," Patricia answered. She had just arrived on the island herself and she didn't know where *anything* was. Patricia asked why in the world a young girl like herself would want to know where a pawn shop was. Casey told her that her grandmother had died "a couple of months ago" and had left her some jewelry, and she wanted to pawn it. Patricia expressed her dismay of her wanting to get rid of a family heirloom. She told Casey that both her grandmothers were dead and that she would never part with anything they had given her. Why would Casey ever do such a thing? She said it was because they had no money and no place to stay.

Casey showed Patricia the jewelry. After inspecting the gold bracelet and necklace, the older woman handed it back to her, saying she was sorry she couldn't help her. Patricia walked out of the room to find Brian. She cornered him in his room.

Patricia told her elder son that there was something not right about these girls and to "get them the hell out" of her house. She told Brian she thought the girls were runaways and that they had stolen the jewelry. She smelled trouble and she wanted them *out*.

Patricia observed that Krystal was "really, really quiet." She seemed very insecure and "clinging." Casey was just the opposite. She was obviously the one in charge.

The phone in the house and the family's cell phones had not been activated yet, so Patricia asked Holly if she could use hers. She spent the next forty-five minutes on the phone activating her cell. It was toward the end of her conversation with the service provider when she began to hear the sounds of a helicopter. She went outside to look and saw it flying over the house. It was now about 11:00 AM.

Inside the house Brian and Brett noticed that Casey and Krystal looked at each other with frightened faces when they realized the helicopter was just overhead. They then got "real quiet." As soon as the boys left the room, they began hearing the girls nervously whispering to each other.

Patricia had to go out and take care of house business and told her sons that if they needed her, to call her on the cell phone.

EIGHT

Once the US Marshals' tracking system pinpointed the Colliers' stolen cell phone location out on Tybee Island, two Marshals from the Savannah office made the short drive down to the beach resort. The barrier island, just eighteen miles east of Savannah, is only three miles long and the Marshals believed they would have no difficulty locating the two fugitives. Tybee Road was the only way on and off the island. If there ever was an ideal location to capture wanted felons, you would have to look hard to find a better trap than Tybee.

The Marshals then proceeded to cruise the beach area and within minutes located the parked, hard-to-miss indigo blue 2002 Chevrolet Silverado extended-cab truck. The license plates were a match to the missing vehicle. The truck belonged to Carl Collier.

Turner and McElwaney were in constant voice communication with the Marshals and their boss Bruce Jordan, who was en route to the ocean-fronting island by helicopter. They would await the arrival of Jordan before any attempt to apprehend the two teenagers.

Arriving at 8:40 AM, Detectives Turner and McElwaney were met by members of the SERFTF team and the Tybee Island Police Department.

The Tybee Island police were asked to assist the Marshals and the Fayette County sheriff's detectives in the apprehension of the two suspects. Due to their size and lack of experience in such cases, the small seventeen-man police force had agreed to take the back seat on the operation even though it was in their jurisdiction.

Bruce Jordan's helicopter touched down next to the Tybee Island lighthouse at approximately 11:15 AM. Despite the disparate locations of all involved in the upcoming bust, the timing couldn't have been better. Now a strategy for apprehending the suspects had to be mapped out. It would take several more hours for the US Marshal Service's tracking system, *Stingray*, to hone in on the exact position of the fugitives' cell phone signal.

The Marshals had finally pinpointed the signal of the target cell phone to three adjacent beach houses. All three were typical of the popular beach playground: packed in like sardines on the valuable waterfront property. Although the *Stingray* tracking system was incredibly accurate, the Marshals, after an hour of trying, couldn't be sure which one of the houses the girls were holed up in. Jordan was losing patience and felt they couldn't afford any more delay. He positioned himself in front of the homes and ordered the assembled force of eighteen police to mount their raid. It was 1:50 PM.

Dodie Gay was in the bathroom on her knees running some water into a bucket with soap. She was tidying up her furniture-bare house in anticipation of the arrival of a new tenant. Suddenly she heard voices and heavy footsteps running up the wooden staircase on the side of her house to the raised living quarters at 16 Bright Street. Moments later she heard banging and male voices demanding she open the door. Frightened, she fumbled with the door knob with soapy hands. Finally succeeding in opening the door, she was shocked to see four men in black fatigues crouched behind their Department of Justice body shields. They were all pointing guns at her. She couldn't help but focus on the red combat sights at the ends of the gun barrels, thinking she'd better not excite these guys, and hoping that they hadn't drunk too much coffee that day.

She immediately shot her arms above her head and dropped to her knees, then lay face down on her living room floor. Dodie Gay was not a very threatening figure. Just 5'4" inches tall, the forty-something mother was wearing a baseball cap, shorts, and a Lifeline for Children T-shirt that read "I Put Kids First." The law enforcement men demanded to know who she was and if anyone else was in the house. After a quick search, the battle-ready policemen flashed a picture of a young girl in front of the face of the still-prostrated woman. Dodie Gay replied that she had never seen the girl. Ironically Gay was a juvenile probation officer and a director of the Crime Stoppers program in Savannah, so she knew the drill. After a few minutes, the men, realizing they were in the wrong house, apologized and departed without a word of explanation, leaving the shaken and perplexed woman still stretched out face down on her living room floor.

Gay finally got to her feet and went out on the screened porch overlooking her driveway. It was full of police cars with flashing lights. She stood back and watched the unfolding drama.

Along with the two girls, Brett watched the raid on his next-door neighbor's house from his bedroom window in the back. The girls looked panicky. He quickly put two and two together. The cops were at the wrong house! They were looking for the girls. Brett sprinted out of the room and down the stairs to the carports and then out front and hollered to the cops: were they looking for the girls? Bruce Jordan, in as firm a voice as he could muster, screamed back, "Where the girls at?"

The excited boy blurted out "They're here! We just met them on the beach last night."

The assembled force piled into the house. They quickly encountered Brett in the first-floor living area above the garage ports and pointed their guns at him. He could see the red beams of the laser sights pointing at his forehead. The cops ordered him to the floor. Moments later, Brian walked into the suddenly crowded room. The laser beam sights now were pointed at him. The cops demanded to know where the girls were. Brian pointed to the back bedroom door. Ordering him to join his brother on the floor, the force of lawmen leapt over the prone brothers and stormed to the back and broke open the closed door.

The frightened Holly Harvey and Sandy Ketchum were found holding each other in the small bedroom. The teenage lovers were quickly handcuffed and thrown down onto the mattress on their stomachs. Holly was wearing shorts and a tee-shirt. Sandy had on a long-sleeve shirt and jeans.

Bruce Jordan walked into the room and told the girls that they were under arrest for the murders of Carl and Sarah Collier. He rolled Sandy over on her back to handcuff her and was surprised to see a knife protruding from each pocket. He remembers thinking the girl was lucky she didn't stab herself.

Jordan then straddled Holly to restrain the squirming, handcuffed teenager and punched in the number for Sheriff Randall Johnson on his cell phone. When the veteran lawman answered, Jordan simply said, "We got 'em." Jordan then noticed Holly trying to slip her wrist out of the handcuffs. Jordan had to drop all his weight on her to prevent her from freeing herself. He told her, "You ain't fighting with your grandma now, so just settle down."

Surveying the sparsely furnished room, Jordan saw a set of car keys lying at the foot of the mattress. He asked the girls if they were the ones to the truck. They kept their mouths shut. The two were stood up and walked out of the room. Because the room was small, only four officers had entered to subdue the pair. Further looking around the room, Jordan could plainly see a bloody fingerprint smudge. At the head of the mattress was a prescription bottle for Adderall with

Holly's name on it. Beside Holly on the floor was a small jewelry bag containing a gold nugget necklace and a gold tennis bracelet.

Jordan asked Tybee police officer Corporal Tiffany Wall to search the two suspects. She searched Sandy first and found only two cigarette lighters and a blue wallet in her pockets. Holly had nothing in her possession.

When they were led downstairs, Holly seemed surprised how many policemen were in the house. She became giddy from all the attention, and even let out a laugh. Bruce Jordan was taken aback by her demeanor. He thought he was looking at the devil incarnate.

Detective Bo Turner was standing on the side of the cascading staircase that dropped down from the front porch to the sand. There were another dozen lawmen lining the banisters with him. As Holly was being led down the stairs with her hands cuffed, she spotted Turner. The expression on her face told him that she had recognized him, no doubt from the confrontation a few weeks before when Turner and McElwaney had caught up with her at Sandy's house after she'd run away.

As Holly stared at him, she smirked, as if saying, "Look at me and all the attention I'm getting." It gave Turner an eerie feeling.

As Jordan escorted Sandy to a transport vehicle, he asked her if she intended to tell him the truth about what had happened. Sandy looked at him with her sad brown eyes and said, "Yes, I'll tell you the truth."

The Tybee Island police station was just a three-minute drive away. The station, like the island police force, was small. Tybee Police Officers Frederick Anderson and Kevin Coursey booked the two disheveled teens. After fingerprinting them and finishing the paperwork, Holly asked the two officers if they were involved in her case. They told her no. She then asked, "Did they die all the way?" Officer Anderson asked what she was referring to. Holly answered by saying, "You must not know anything about my case."

The interview room was no larger than 10' × 10' and had only two desks. Jordan started the interrogation of Sandy Ketchum at about 3:00 PM. Corporal Tiffany Wall was asked to sit in for the interview.

Jordan read Sandy her rights and when asked if she understood them, she meekly answered "Yes." Jordan then asked her if she would answer some questions. She again answered in the affirmative, her voice just above a whisper. When asked if she was under the influence of any substance, Sandy admitted taking an "unknown pill" at around 4:00 AM, but she was now clear-headed and understood the questions she was being asked. Jordan continued with the interrogation. The interview was over in twenty-three minutes.

Holly was walked into the room by Tybee Police Officer April Smith. Jordan, sitting on the edge of the desk, put his palms up and said, "Whoa, don't sit her down!" Jordan stared hard at the defiant teenager in front of him and in a sharp clipped voice said, "Are you going to talk to me?" Exchanging the venomous glance, she replied, "No." "Good, you little bitch," said Jordan. "I don't want to talk to you either, because I'm gonna send you down the river." That was the end of the interrogation of Holly Harvey.

A detective from Tybee Island PD asked that someone from the task force brief the chief of the island police force. Jordan immediately volunteered. Just prior to the interrogations of the suspects, Jordan had gone to see Chief James Price, apologized for the lack of communication with the department, and explained the whole operation. According to Jordan the chief was "very understanding" and assured Jordan that no egos had been stepped on.

By the time Holly and Sandy were escorted off the island it was 4 PM. Detective Bo Turner realized it had been almost twelve hours since he had eaten, and that was just a sandwich his wife had packed for him when he and McElwaney left for the airport. The hungry and exhausted detective couldn't remember the last time he had slept. Turner mentioned that he was famished and was immediately seconded by the rest of the police contingent. Jordan suggested dinner at the nearby Savannah Shrimp Co., and all the men nodded their heads enthusiastically.

As the Fayette County policemen and US Marshals, fifteen in all, unwound over the sumptuous meal, there was a tangible sense of elation. The men were in a jovial mood and the officers swapped stories and marveled over the fact that the bust had gone off without a hitch. Everything had been by the book. It was perfectly executed police work, where the fugitives were identified, located, and captured—and all within seventeen hours.

Just maybe, Jordan thought, they had thwarted another horrendous crime by their timely arrival on Tybee Island. Holly and Sandy, AKA Casey and Krystal to Brett and Brian and their mother, Patricia, were desperate for cash and an escape vehicle. Jordan believed they were waiting for Mrs. Pelierin to return from town with money and her car before killing the entire family. That would explain the knife in Sandy's front pocket when she was arrested. Two homicides could easily have become five if not for *Stingray* and some good old-fashioned police work. For once, everything had fallen into place. Bruce Jordan smiled at his good fortune. He picked up the $400 dinner tab.

Jordan was glad that his first hunch, which had had them headed for Daytona Beach in neighboring Florida, had been wrong. Had they crossed into Florida and been captured there, a potentially lengthy extradition process would have to have been initiated. Because the girls had fled to a Georgia beach, they were now in the custody of the authorities from the jurisdiction where the crimes were committed. That was a stroke of luck.

Holly Harvey and Sandy Ketchum were taken to the 1,400-inmate–capacity Chatham County Jail in Savannah, which had a juvenile facility within its walls. Jordan arranged the overnight for the two suspects. They'd be transported back to Fayetteville the next morning.

When questioned by the admitting officer, Lieutenant Brenda Washington, on why she was there, Holly replied: "I killed my grandma and grandpa. At least, I think they died."

Due to the heinous nature of the charges and the high visibility of the case, the two girls were examined by prison psychologist June Stewart in the prison's juvenile center that evening. Holly was tearful throughout the interview. When Stewart asked her if she knew why she was locked up, she replied, "I killed my grandma and grandpa." She then related that there had been "blood everywhere," and that she remembered seeing a knife. Holly told the prison shrink that she had been living with her grandparents for the past two to three months, and prior to that she was living with a friend's mom, Connie Earwood. Her mom, Carla, was presently in jail for selling marijuana to an undercover police officer, and she never saw her father, (As told to the prison psychologist by Holly) who was now living with his dad after burning his home down after smoking crack. Holly told Stewart that she had been angry with her grandparents, but wouldn't elaborate. She did, however, state that her grandparents had been "hitting me" and that she was defending herself when she stabbed them.

Holly also admitted to a habit of smoking fifteen to twenty marijuana blunts (cigarettes) a day. She also said she had smoked some crack over the weekend, but that she'd smoked it unwittingly because somebody had put it in her blunt. She explained away her marijuana habit by saying that she "likes the way she feels when she uses it" and didn't consider it abuse. She claimed to have attempted suicide in the past, the last time just a year ago when she'd cut her wrist, but that no stitches were required. Stewart then reported that Holly had told her she was scheduled for a counseling session over a purported bi-polar disorder. Stewart asked the teenager what she thought of that. Holly answered, "I think it's bullshit."

Holly also complained of problems sleeping and recurrent nightmares, the last one three weeks earlier where she'd dreamt that she had pushed an old lady "who fell and busted her head." She went on to say that in her dream "the blood was all over her and a nurse gave her something." Holly looked up, puzzled, and said, "Maybe I knew I was going to kill my grandma."

Delving into her psyche, Stewart got Holly to admit that she got angry and got into fights when she was provoked. Stewart asked her if she knew when to stop, and Holly answered, "Yes, but I don't always do." The interview ended with Holly sadly assuming she would be locked up for the rest of her life and would probably "die for what she had done."

In her report, Stewart listed Holly Harvey's thought process as "restlessness," no delusional beliefs, an "anxious" mood, and "cooperative" in manner. Holly also had a persistent cannabis substance disorder and an adolescent onset of conduct disorder. She was deemed not a suicide risk, but Stewart recommended a prescription "if applicable" of the amphetamine Adderall.

Carlitha Givens performed the mental health assessment on Sandy Ketchum at 9:21 PM. Sandy quickly admitted to extensive substance abuse problems, and that she couldn't remember if she'd been high when she committed the crimes she was there for. She did confess to smoking marijuana laced with cocaine the night before the murders. She didn't really remember the events of the afternoon of August 2, other than "everything happened so fast."

In tears, she wailed that she wished she were dead "so that she didn't have to deal with this mess," and that she had given up hope for her life and wanted to kill herself. When pressed how she would do it, she answered that she didn't know, but it would be "the quickest" way.

Sandy rambled on about suicide, admitting to overdosing on some drugs two summers ago, but she didn't remember why. She had also cut herself about nine times with a knife, usually on her wrist. Sandy had undergone counseling after the overdose, but hadn't had any since. She had been put on Risperdal for her sleeping problems, Depakote for her bi-polar disorder, and Paxil for depression. Sandy complained that she'd had trouble sleeping for a year and the Risperdal was not helping, so her stepmother had taken her off it.

The 16-year-old said she had a good relationship with her dad but not her step-mom, saying she got easily upset "when her parents say things to her." She claimed her step-mom had called her a bitch and that "she would knock her [Sandy's] teeth down her throat." Her parents were always telling her "she would never be anything, and that she is going to be trash just like her [natural] mother."

Sandy told Givens that she had never known her mother until just recently "when she found her." Her second mother had beaten her. She had told her dad, but he did not believe her. Sandy said that she had even gotten pictures taken of her bruises to show her dad evidence of the abuse, and that he still didn't believe her.

She claimed that it wasn't until he had felt mistreated by his second wife that he'd left her. Sandy said she still had "bad dreams and thoughts" about her step-mother's abuse. Apparently Sandy was speaking of her third mother, second stepmother. She had no real memory of her first stepmother and therefore did not count her in the mental health assessment.

Sandy admitted to losing her temper easily when people aggravated her, and reported that she'd crushed her knuckles on a cement wall once when she was mad. She was easily frustrated when she couldn't do things right. Sandy had problems concentrating, and it was easy for her "to wander off." She denied hearing voices, but admitted to hearing music in her head that other people couldn't hear. Her chest always hurt and she had terrible headaches. Sandy told Givens that cur-rently charges were pending against her for "Unruly and Ungovernable Conduct."

Givens found Sandy to have a logical and coherent thought process, no delusional beliefs but audio hallu-cinations. Her manner was "cooperative." The prison analyst recommended that the youth be placed in her room with a suicide-proof vest, a suicide-proof blan-ket, a mattress, and a pillow. Guards were instructed to search her every time she left or returned to her cell.

Holly Harvey and Sandy Ketchum were loaded into two separate SUVs for the 250-mile drive back to Fayetteville. Two female officers, Sergeant Tracey Carroll and Sergeant Lenelle Coker, accompanied Sandy and Holly respectively. Harvey didn't utter a word on the four-hour drive. Ketchum, on the other hand, was talkative, and continually broke into crying fits. She kept saying how she kept "smelling blood" and how she was "reliving it every five minutes" and "those people didn't deserve to die."

Lieutenant Mahlon Donald sat in the front seat of Ketchum's vehicle. Donald, who was the Fayette County officer attached to SERFTF, listened as Sandy spoke tearfully of how she wanted to write a book. Donald pointed out that, if convicted of a felony, she wouldn't profit from any book on her crime. Sandy answered by saying that she just wanted to write a book of poetry. It was a sad reminder to Donald that the two captured murderers were just kids, naïve in many ways.

Arriving at the Fayette County Sheriff's Office, Sandy and Holly were photographed and fingerprinted by Crime Scene Investigator Manny Rojas. Sandy was then turned over to the warrant division and was transported to the Atlanta Metro Regional Youth Detention Center without incident. Holly was taken to the Clayton County Regional Youth Detention Center in nearby Lovejoy.

Beth and Tim were staying with friends in Griffin. On the afternoon of August 3, Beth informed the Spalding County sheriff's deputies guarding the house that she and her husband had to leave to pick up some prescription medication for him. The police refused to let them go, but Beth was persistent. The sheriff's deputies finally relented and the distraught couple drove off. Just after 3 PM they heard the report on the car radio that Holly and their daughter Sandy had been captured on

Tybee Island. In silence the couple drove home to Franklin.

At 10:00 AM on Wednesday, August 4, at an impound lot on Tybee, Bruce Jordan, Crime Scene Investigators Manny Rojas and Josh Shelton, and Detective Ethon Harper began inventorying the contents of the blue Silverado that had belonged to Carl Collier. In the back seat Jordan found a blue-and-clear plastic backpack. Inside, mixed with bloody clothes, Jordan noticed a bundled towel. Wearing latex gloves, he removed and unwrapped it. Just as Sandy had said he would the day before at the Tybee Island police station, he found two large kitchen knives encrusted with dried blood.

The US Marshals returned to the house at 18 Bright Street to question Patricia and her sons Brian and Brett. The cops told them they thought the newly arrived family would have been the girls' next victims. They theorized that the girls would have robbed them, murdered them, and stolen their vehicle.

On Thursday the Fayette County detectives paid them a visit. The detectives questioned each of them separately and then together. The tone the police took, according to Patricia Palleirin, was as if they were dealing with hardened criminals because Sandy Ketchum had confessed that she, Holly, and the Clayton brothers had all smoked pot. The detectives wondered out loud why the boys would let these "horrible" girls into their house. Patricia defended them by saying they'd had no idea what they had done, and that they'd felt sorry for them and were only trying to do the right thing by giving shelter to two apparent runaways. Patricia said her boys were being "perfect gentlemen" with no intention of soliciting sexual favors from the two fugitives.

The cops insisted that Brian knew that the girls had killed Holly's grandparents. Brian vehemently denied any such knowledge, and said if he'd known, he would have called the cops immediately. It was a humiliating experience, and upset Patricia greatly. They were law-abiding citizens, so how could these cops sitting in her living room turn that around on them? Patricia asked how police could make her and her family out to be "the bad guys" when the girls they had in custody were "homicidal maniacs."

When the first media frenzy hit the Fayette County Sheriff's Office the day of the girls' capture, Jordan had agreed to appear on ABC's *Good Morning America* with the victims' son, Kevin Collier, to discuss the preliminary facts on the case. Anchor Diane Sawyer would be conducting the interview from New York. That night Jordan got a phone call from the show's producer saying Kevin Collier would not be appearing with him.

Arriving at the studio Jordan noticed two chairs set up in front of the cameras. He asked who would occupy the second chair. The producers told him they would also be interviewing Sara Polk, the young girl who had alerted the police initially about the murders. "Not sitting next to me you won't," Jordan had replied.

Jordan had not yet had a chance to interview the teenage friend of the suspects, and wasn't even sure if she had told his detectives the whole story of Holly and Sandy's visit to her house in Griffin where they had confessed to the murders. As Jordan related, "The smoke hadn't cleared yet, and it would have been unethical for me to sit there with one of the key witnesses on nationwide TV before any trial."

The producer rushed to a phone and called the program's New York–based executive producer. Jordan was put on the phone. New York pleaded with him to do the interview with Polk. Jordan explained that the situation was "a deal breaker." A decision was made to put Sara Polk in a car and drive her over to another studio in Atlanta. The pair was interviewed by Diane Sawyer simultaneously, albeit miles apart.

NINE

An autopsy was performed by Chief Medical Examiner Kris Sperry on the body of Carl Collier at the Georgia Bureau of Investigation, Division of Forensic Sciences, in Atlanta, on August 3, 2004, commencing at 9:45 AM, pursuant to the Georgia Death Investigation Act.

The external investigation concluded that the body that lay on the morgue slab was that of a "well nourished elderly Caucasian male, who weighs 155 pounds, is 70 inches in height, and appears compatible with the stated age of 74 years."

Carl Collier had been dressed in a sleeveless ribbed undershirt, which was "heavily saturated with liquid and clotted blood." On the upper right front of the shirt was an oval hole that corresponded to a stab wound to the chest. Carl Collier's blue denim trousers were soaked in urine and blood.

On closer examination Dr. Sperry found a superficial knife wound on Mr. Collier's supraorbital ridge (brow). His right ear was partially amputated. On the right lateral side of his head, extending down to his neck, was a 6.5 cm, slashing wound.

On the upper surface of the right shoulder, at the base of the neck, were a total of "four superficial incisions" which varied from 2.5 cm to 6.5 cm in length. The neck had a more serious wound.

The "gaping wound" that began at the left mid-clavical extended inward 5.7 cm across and down. The wound had struck the first thoracic vertebra (mid-spinal region), notching it. It had also opened the carotid artery, "creating a gaping, massively hemorrhagic" 3 cm wound. The track of the knife sliced into the esophagus and the trachea and down into the hilar (upper) region of the right lung, which was also extensively hemorrhagic. The right pleural (lung) cavity contained approximately 200 ml of blood.

Another stab wound was found in the mid-sternal region, slightly to the right of the midline. A slashing wound was found on the left shoulder that stretched 9.7 cm in length. Several more superficial and non-threatening wounds were found in this area. But on the upper right thorax (back of lung), below the base of the neck, was a gaping teardrop-shaped incision. It extended towards the base of the neck for almost 3 inches.

On Carl Collier's left shoulder and back, four more knife wounds were found. Three more were located on his left arm and hand. Dr. Sperry also found a defensive knife wound on Carl Collier's left hand.

A total of eight superficial and deep stab wounds to the face, head, and neck, and nine more in his chest and back area all contributed to death by exsanguination.

According to the chief medical examiner's report, the coup de grace was the wound that had penetrated into his left neck, incising the aorta, which had led to massive internal and external hemorrhaging.

In laymen's terms, Carl Collier had bled to death from multiple stab wounds.

An autopsy of Sarah Collier followed her husband's at 11:35 AM.

Sarah Collier was "a well nourished adult Caucasian female, who weighed 180 pounds, was 63 inches in height, compatible with the stated age of 73 years."

Her Hawaiian floral print shirt was saturated with blood, with one very large, gaping hole that corresponded to a stab wound. Her white brassiere exhibited "incised defects," which also corresponded to stab wound injuries.

Collier's floral print shorts were heavily bloodstained and had defects associated with stab wound injuries.

On the lateral left neck, below the angle of the jaw, was a horizontally oriented, 3.3 cm stab wound incision. On the right parietal scalp (back of head) was a stab wound that had perforated the right parietal bone into the cranial vault, slightly penetrating the brain.

On the right breast, above the nipple, was a 4.5 cm stab wound incision that extended deeply into the tissues of the breast. On the upper right breast was a large, gaping stab wound, which measured 13 cm in length. The margins of the wound were focally irregular, "reflecting removal of the blade and reinsertion, during the course of the infliction of this wound."

On the mid anterior thorax (chest) was an inverted

angulated gaping stab wound, measuring 13 cm in length. On the right lower abdomen was a large 6.5 cm stab wound. The stab wound penetrated the fat into the peritoneal cavity (gut) resulting in mesenteric hemorrhaging (intestinal bleeding). Overlying the right lateral inguinal region (lower gut) was a 2.3 cm stab wound. In the lateral mid right abdomen region were two more superficial punctures. Just above it was another.

On the right posterior mid-thoracic area (mid-back) was a deep stab wound which measured 5.5 cm in length. The knife had penetrated into the thoracic cavity, notching the right tenth rib. The track incised the lower lobe of the right lung.

On Sarah Collier's upper left arm was a deep, gaping, 7.5 cm stab wound that pierced the arm. Another stab wound was found on the left forearm, as were two more superficial defensive wounds on the left hand.

At the juncture of the right arm with the left shoulder, anteriorly, was a large, 6 cm stab wound that transected the axillary (below shoulder) artery, causing massive hemorrhaging that had led to exsanguination. On the right posterolateral (side) upper arm, three more stab wounds were found.

On the dorsal right forearm was an obliquely oriented deep slash wound, measuring 11.5 cm, that had penetrated deep into the musculature and severed numerous tendons. Two more stab wounds were located on the right hand.

On the posterior right upper arm, adjacent to the shoulder articulation, a large, gaping stab wound measuring 6.2 cm was found. The wound extended deeply into the musculature and soft tissue of the posterior arm and shoulder. Another superficial stab wound measuring 4.4 cm in length was discovered on the posterior mid right upper arm.

Chief Medical Examiner Kris Sperry concluded that Sarah Collier had sustained multiple stab wounds of the head, neck, chest, and abdomen, and right and left upper arms. The wound that had entered the right shoulder, transecting the right axillary artery, led to the "massive exsanguinating hemorrhage and her death."

The manner of death, concluded Sperry, like that of her husband's, was homicide.

TEN

After her return to Fayetteville and her lock-up in the Metro RYDC, Sandy Ketchum placed a phone call to her parents. Her dad answered the call, but was overcome with emotion on hearing his little girl's voice. Sobbing, he handed the phone to Beth.

"Mommy," came the frightened voice over the line. Beth asked her how she was doing. Sandy didn't answer for several moments, finally saying she "didn't kill nobody."

Beth told her she "was in a lot of trouble," adding ". . . and you ain't gonna be gettin' outta this."

Beth told her the brutal truth. "I had fixed, and gotten you out of all the trouble you had gotten into before, and paid your way out of everything you gotten into before, but money ain't gonna buy your way outta this. I don't understand, I don't know what happened, but you're in this thing for the long haul."

Sandy, in a tearful voice, asked Beth if she still loved her. Beth assured her that she still did. Sandy then asked if they would "be sticking by" her.

Beth said yes again, but added, "Under one condition—you're gonna have to tell me what happened, because I can't support you until you do. I wanna know what in the hell went wrong, since that's the only way I can help ya."

Sandy told her step-mom that she had been over at Holly's house and "we were doing drugs and things got out of hand, and Holly's grandparents got kilt and we stole Holly's grandfather's truck and ran and we got picked up."

Beth asked Sandy if she'd killed anybody. Sandy said no. Beth asked her to explain. Sandy said that Holly and her grandmother had gotten into an argument. Her grandfather had come down to the basement bedroom and both of them had gotten on top of Holly. Holly had hollered for help. Sandy had then jumped up from behind the bed where she'd been hiding, and saw Holly stabbing her grandmother. Sandy had gotten into a "wrestling match with them" and tried to take the knife away from Holly. Holly was under her grandmother and began screaming that she couldn't breathe, and to get her grandmother off her. Sandy then said she'd [Sandy] stabbed Sarah Collier in the arm and in the back of the head—but didn't kill her. Holly had then chased her grandfather upstairs and Sandy heard "all the hollering and screaming." She'd gone up to see what was happening, and when she ran into the kitchen, Mr. Collier had seen her and thrown a coffee cup at her, which she ducked. It missed and smashed into pieces against a wall. Then Holly had stabbed him "one more time in the neck and he fell to the floor, dead."

When the two girls returned to the basement, they'd found Mrs. Collier at the foot of the stairs. Holly had then started screaming at Sandy that she was not dead, since she was still breathing. Sandy'd cried, "No, no, no" and that she *was* dead. Holly began stabbing her grandmother, screaming "This fat bitch won't die," making sure that Sarah Collier was dead. Sandy and Holly then quickly packed up and left.

Sandy claimed to remember little after that. The shock of what had happened and the self-induced drug haze she'd been in had made the events following the deaths of Carl and Sarah Collier a blur.

Tim Ketchum was, by his own admission, in a daze himself, but it wasn't drug-induced. It was the shock from the enormity of what his little girl had done. They had little money and no idea of where to turn for legal help.

Sandy had always taken to the pen and paper to express herself. She began to write prolifically in verse and letter form. Within days Tim and Beth Ketchum received two revealing poems.

"FEELING REMORSE"

Feeling remorse,
For the one I hurt.
Wanting to die,
And be put in the dirt.

Hearing the discrete sound,
And smelling the awful smell.

Nowhere to be found,
Am I going to hell?

Losing my mind,
Not knowing what to do.
Falling behind,
Every time I look at you.

Knowing that they're dead,
And I can't bring them back.
It replays in my head,
And makes a big impact.

Sandy Ketchum
August 13, 2004

"ONE BAD EXPERIENCE"

When I was on the outside,
Doing drugs everyday.
I was just along for the ride,
And in one spot, I would never stay.

Going in an out,
Not wanting to ever wake.
They finally found out.
That my problem wasn't fake.

Finding me in the floor,
Almost ready to die.
I was scratching at the door,
When I heard my father cry.

I had ten minutes left,
With everything flashing before my eyes.
I almost took my life,
I was ready for my own demise.

The next few moments,
Were quite a haze.
When they rushed me in,
I was out in a daze.

I couldn't feed myself,
And didn't know who I was.
After this, they asked me "why,"
And I said "just because."

I was tired of feeling pain,
And crying every night.
I just felt so alone,
Like I couldn't win any fight.

Now I really see,
It wasn't my time to go.
But to my parents,
I want to say "thank you" though.

Sandy Ketchum
August 26, 2004

ELEVEN

A graduate of Harvard University and the University of South Carolina Law School, Idaho native Lloyd Walker's career started in the corporate offices of an Atlanta law firm that specialized in construction litigation. It wasn't long before he, and his company, discovered that his heart was not in corporate law. Like many idealistic children of the 1960s, Walker found corporate work uninspiring, and it had him yearning for work that could be deemed more meaningful.

A lawyer friend in Walker's adopted home town of Peachtree City, in Fayette County, who was a public defender, encouraged him to join his practice and share his lofty goal of protecting the rights of the indigent. Walker didn't have to think twice about leaving his office tower cubicle for the leafy semi-rural suburbs he now calls home. The portly, soft-spoken transplant from the mountainous western regions hung up his shingle and became a trial attorney dedicated to defending society's cast-offs.

It was not particularly lucrative, but it was rewarding work. Walker relished ensuring due process for citizens who had limited access to "the American Dream." He supplemented his modest compensation from the state of Georgia by handling the usual small-town legal work: suits, divorces, custody cases, and real estate in Fayette County. Occasionally there were even the juicy lawsuits against corporate America that he could sink his teeth into. Lloyd Walker relished the role of a Don Quixote taking on the plutocracy that he perceived ran America as much as he did sparring with the conservative legal system of the state of Georgia on behalf of those who couldn't afford to pay for legal counsel.

Walker brought strong beliefs with him to the defense table. He believed that you can't be an effective defense attorney if you are afraid of the courtroom, though the truth of the matter was, about 90 percent of cases were settled in plea bargains. But to be taken seriously by the other side, the district attorney's office, you had better be ready "to mix it up in front of the bench." If the prosecutors got wind of any defense reluctance to go to trial, you wouldn't get the generous plea offers—or respect. Lloyd Walker got the respect of the Fayette County District Attorney's Office.

Along with fellow lawyer Judy Chidester, Walker is a member of the Indigent Defense Committee for the Griffin Judicial District, which encompasses Fayette, Spalding, Pike, and Upson counties. The job of the committee is to appoint attorneys for all indigents—or those unable to afford legal counsel—being tried criminally in the four jurisdictions. The bulk of the cases Walker handled were in the juvenile division: delinquent actions by children and parent deprivation acts.

On August 3, 2004, Walker was in juvenile court talking to other lawyers about the murders of Carl and Sarah Collier the night before. From the legal scuttlebutt in the courthouse, he learned that one of the suspects was Sandy Ketchum, a client of his from juvenile court. Walker culled his memory and remembered that he was representing her on a charge that had still not been adjudicated. Technically he was still her attorney of record. As a good defense lawyer, he immediately realized that there might be a good case for throwing out anything she might have said while in custody, since he, her attorney, had not been there to represent her. Walker was of the firm belief that the district attorneys and the courts had to follow due process to prove *their* cases, and it was his job to see to it that they did. It was how the judicial system in America was designed to work, innocent until proven guilty.

It was the inability of some of the public to understand that brought up the inevitable questions, such as how he could defend a criminal like Sandy Ketchum. Walker's answer would be that after years before the bench, you learn how powerful the state is and how arbitrary and capricious it can be. It then becomes the defense attorney's job to make sure that the state follows the rules if they are intent on taking the life, the liberty, or the property of his client. A competent defense lawyer has to make sure that it is done according to the laws and the Constitution of this country and those of the state of Georgia.

Lloyd Walker did not lose any sleep over the prospect of putting a guilty person back on the street. He saw it as the inability of the state to prove its case. That was how the system worked. The public, Walker believed, often wants to cut corners and rush to decision and punish the alleged offenders, but that belief quickly goes out the window when it is one of them being arrested and questioned about something that might result in their loss of liberty or life.

It was these deeply held beliefs that had him and public defender and colleague Judy Chidester assigning the cases of Holly Harvey and Sandy Ketchum to themselves when it became apparent that the two teens and their families did not have the financial wherewithal to hire high-powered defense attorneys of their own. Chidester would handle Holly Harvey and Walker would assume Sandy Ketchum's defense.

Sandy and her parents still held out hope that they could get some high-powered defense attorney to help. On an AOL Hometown they made a plea for donations to her defense. It was titled "Sandra Ketchum's Plea for Help."

After a brief biography of the 16-year old, the web page launched into "Sandy's Cry for Help."

My name is Sandy Ketchum. As many of you may know, I have made some poor decisions and must answer for my actions. I deeply regret the situation I am in and the people who I have hurt including my family. I am willing to take full responsibility and face the legal consequences but I need legal assistance. My family is not able to provide legal council so I am writing this letter to ask for your help. Anything you can do would be greatly appreciated.

Sincerely,
Sandy Ketchum

The desperate plea for help was followed by a statement from Tim and Beth Ketchum titled "The Family of Sandy Ketchum Speaks Out."

Our hearts have been ripped from our very souls. As you read the newspapers and watch the news, please remember that some of it is true and some is not. You will have to decide what to believe. Listen to our child's words as we have chosen to do. To go through something like this, well, there is only one emotion. Your heart is torn from your soul and the world is no longer there. There is no place to go . . . we can't go back so we must go forward. We put our faith in God and ask for his guidance. Our prayers are with anyone who has ever had to endour [sic] what we are going through. Something like this consumes and eats everything around you. Aunt Pat, Aunt Glinda and their families' hands are held out wide open. However, there is nothing to fill them except love. More love than any of those who judge Sandy will ever understand. Glinda has played a huge part in Sandy's life and given her more love and understanding than most of us will get in a lifetime. She has a grandmother who's [sic] love has no boundaries. Sandy's father and I speak out hoping that somewhere in the world someone hears us and feels our pain. The media eats you alive and spits you out in little pieces. Everyone we know, and have

*known our whole lives asks if there [sic] anything they
can do to help. We are just an average family with very
limited funds. Like most people, we live paycheck to
paycheck. Our jobs have suffered and our life has disappeared. Our only survival is to help our child. We
plea for funds to give our daughter the best representa-
tion we can. One more time, I speak your own words
back to you . . . "is there anything we can do to help?"
Our answer "Yes."*

Thanks for listening and giving us your time.

Any contributions will be greatly appreciated.

*Sincerely,
The Ketchum Family*

Judy Chidester was a home-grown product of the
Georgia legal system. She was a graduate of Georgia
State University and had a 1981 law degree from
Emory University in Atlanta. Chidester is a member of
the Georgia Attorneys For Criminal Defense and is active politically, serving as vice-chairman of the Fayette
County Democratic Party and a member of WIN
(Women In Numbers), which encourages pro-choice
advocates to run for public office. She was proud to
live with the labels as a feminist, liberal, pro-choice
Democrat in a decidedly Republican area of the Deep
South. The 52-year-old grandmother, like her colleague Lloyd Walker, was determined that Holly Harvey would get all the protection of federal and state law
that she was entitled to.

Both Fayette County lawyers knew there would
come a time when their respective clients' interests
would force them to part ways. A common defense

would not be possible. Too much would be at stake.

Judy Chidester reported in *The Citizen* that in her conferences with Holly, the teenager repeatedly asked her, in tears, "Does everybody in the world hate me?" She said that the young girl was "very frightened, very upset, very scared and very emotional." Chidester added, "She seems to be genuinely distraught and remorseful. She appears to me to be a terrified 15-year-old."

According to Chidester, Holly appeared to comprehend most of their private conversations regarding the seriousness of the charges against her, but often the lawyer got the quizzical looks from her that one would expect of a teen, making Chidester wonder if Holly really understood what was happening.

Chidester was right when she ruminated about Holly not having "a lot of cheerleaders at her side." The national and local press harped on the grotesqueness of the crimes, and the prurient nature of the girls' sexual orientation. They portrayed the girls as being cold-blooded killers, and not the troubled, scared kids the defense knew them to be.

In its September 20, 2004, edition, *People* magazine made the Colliers' murders their top crime story. "Killer Grandkid?" was the headline, with the underlying copy reading: "Holly Harvey's grandparents tried to save her. Instead, police say, the teen and a friend murdered them."

The article told how the "rebellious 15-year-old" had threatened her grandparents and how, five days later, "the blood-soaked bodies" were found. The much-written-about, but uncorroborated, "Kill, keys, money, jewelry," supposedly seen on Holly's arm in ink got mention. The reporter wrote about how Holly "began to rival her mother in her wild ways" and how she became "romantically involved" with Sandy Ketchum. He went on to explain how Holly "couldn't live under the rules—come home each night, no drinking, no smoking pot or cigarettes in the house—[which] weren't that strict."

Most sensational—and prejudicial—was the description of the murders: "She [Holly] attacked her grandmother with a kitchen knife while Sandy, who'd been lying in wait, leaped out to help Holly."

The popular, widely circulated magazine quoted Sandy as telling police, "I finished with Mrs. Collier then went to join Holly—who had chased her grandfather up the stairs."

The article also quoted Lieutenant Colonel Bruce Jordan as saying, "Holly laughed as she was arrested. She was callous and cocky."

Nationally syndicated radio talk show host Neal Boortz, operating out of Atlanta's WSB, proudly touts himself as the preacher of "the church of the painful truth," and relishes the title bestowed on him by former President Bill Clinton as a "preacher of hate." He has 4,000,000 listeners nationwide. He lambasted Holly Harvey on his show and web page as "that psychotic little monster" who should be tried as an adult, adding, "Hopefully she will spend the rest of her miserable life in jail." With this kind of pre-trial publicity it was no wonder the defense attorneys for the two accused teenage murderers worried about them getting a fair trial.

◆ ◆ ◆

Lloyd Walker had a problem with how the Fayette County Sheriff's Office and Lieutenant Colonel Bruce Jordan in particular, distributed what he deemed prejudicial information about the crime to the public. In the days that followed the capture and arrest of Holly Harvey and Sandy Ketchum, Bruce Jordan was, in the words of Walker, "way too forthcoming with evidence and information of this case that made it practically impossible to obtain a jury that was untainted by it." According to Walker, it was "way over and above what was necessary for the public to know."

There was also the nagging problem propagated by the major Atlanta daily newspaper, *The Atlanta Journal-Constitution*. The paper had printed as fact an article by Rochelle Carter that said Sandy Ketchum alone had killed Sarah Collier. It was based on an "ambiguous statement" released to the press by Bruce Jordan. Carter had written that when the incident occurred, "Ketchum then came out of her hiding place, knife in hand, to help the girl she loved." According to Walker, "The testimony in the court room [arraignment] did not support those factual assertions by your reporter." He also said the statement attributed to Sandy, and printed in the newspaper, declaring "I finished with Mrs. Collier and went to join Holly," was simply untrue. Sandy had never admitted to killing anyone, nor had she said she'd emerged from her hiding place with "knife in hand." Walker demanded a retraction. He got none.

Lloyd Walker denounced the news media's use of these so-called "experts" who were pontificating about motives and analyzing every little aspect of the case. He suggested that they did not have the facts and consequently were in no position to make any informed decisions. By this careless reporting, they were also prejudicing the jury pool. Walker was not oblivious to the public's right to know, but the "uninformed speculation on behalf of experts is counterproductive."

Walker also foresaw some constitutional questions that would have to be addressed, specifically in regard to whether Sandy Ketchum would be tried as an adult. Did children have constitutional protection under the law, or did the Georgia Legislature have carte blanche to determine trial and sentencing procedures? As of 2004, the U.S. Supreme Court had not ruled on whether minors could be executed for their crimes. Children were not given any special treatment because of age. Walker was already looking ahead to a possible Georgia Supreme Court appeal where he could argue that Sandy Ketchum should receive some constitutional protection due to the fact that she was just 16 years old when the crimes were committed. As a liberal Democrat practicing in a conservative Republican area of the Deep South, he knew he would have his work cut out for him. Walker would have to incorporate that strategy in any state court trial, thereby laying down the groundwork for the appeal.

Walker knew that the seriousness of the charges and the facts surrounding them were unique. While a murder case was just like any other case in most respects, this one was different both psychologically and emotionally.

Walker believed there were mitigating factors in

Sandy's life that should affect her ultimate handling in the Georgia court system. There was no question that she had had a troubled adolescence, but, he related, nothing in her past pointed to anything like this happening.

Delaying tactics were a common defense strategy that Walker planned to employ, but he saw little benefit, since the facts, the evidence, and the witnesses wouldn't be going away. All involved in the case were young and had strong ties to the community.

Walker had to face the reality of the case, but the state would still have to persuade him that the evidence they had did, in fact, exist, and that it had been properly handled and was admissible. All these issues, plus the age question, would have to be addressed before he felt comfortable in negotiating any plea bargain deals that would put Sandy Ketchum in prison for any length of time. The downside of rejecting any plea deal was that if it did go to trial and Sandy lost, she could be looking at three consecutive life sentences (the third life sentence could be imposed for the armed robbery charge—the stealing of Carl Collier's truck). Under current Georgia sentencing guidelines, that translated to at least 42 years behind bars. If Walker could help lessen the impact of how long she would have to stay in prison, then they would have to consider a compromise.

Ultimately it would be up to Sandy, but Walker questioned whether a 16-year-old could rationally make a decision about her life that would have such significant consequences. Did the state have the right to force her to make such a decision when it was open to debate whether she had the capacity to do so? Walker espoused a popular belief in the juvenile criminal justice system that children are more impulsive and less rational in the decision-making process. This dilemma could tie her attorney's hands, and it would be a due process issue, affecting his ability to mount a proper defense in his client's behalf.

Walker and Chidester are firm believers in the jury system, with Walker going so far as to say he'd be willing to take "the first twelve people off the street." Walker would later qualify that by adding that they should have no preconceived notions of guilt and should not have been prejudiced by the media. It was those worrisome preconceived notions of guilt that had both defense attorneys agreeing that a fair, unbiased jury would be impossible to assemble in Fayette County. The public was awash in too many details of the case, and public opinion rested squarely with those in the Fayette County law enforcement community. The trial location would have to be moved elsewhere in the state.

At 10 AM on August 12, 2004, two of the youngest murder suspects on record, Holly Harvey and Sandy Ketchum, were led into a packed courtroom in the ten-year-old Fayette County Courthouse in Fayetteville. Superior Court Judge Paschal English sat on the bench. Four TV news cameras taped the entire proceeding. Friends and family of the suspects sat on opposite sides of the courtroom and watched as the emotionless Holly and teary-eyed Sandy were seated at separate tables in the front of the room beneath the red oak bench and the stern-faced Judge English.

Given the judge's permission to proceed, Sandy's defense attorney, Lloyd Walker, quickly called two witnesses to the stand: Tim and Beth Ketchum.

Tim Ketchum appeared emotionally drained and tired. The 42-year-old, out-of-work truck driver told the sad story of his daughter's life. He went into detail about Sandy's natural mother, who'd deserted her, and the succession of three stepmothers. Ketchum described her second stepmother as "physically abusive" to Sandy and the whole relationship as "bad," saying that the stepmother had "always tried to get Sandy into trouble."

Ketchum related how her fourth mom, his present wife Beth, had a good relationship with Sandy, and how she'd done her best in raising the teen for the past four years. He admitted that Sandy had failed court-ordered drug tests while on probation in Coweta County for running away and obstruction of justice.

Out of exasperation Tim Ketchum told the court that he and Beth had acceded to Sandy's wishes to get to know her real mom, Sandra Maddox. On the advice of Sandy's probation officer, they'd even permitted her to move in with Sandra at her home in Griffin, with the understanding that Sandy was not permitted to see Holly. Tim claimed that Sandra had paid no heed to the warnings and allowed, even made it easy for, the two teenage girls to see each other.

Beth Ketchum took the stand next and under questioning by Lloyd Walker said she had "no major problems" with her stepdaughter. She added, "Sandy and I have always gotten along."

Finished questioning Sandy's latest stepmother,

Lloyd Walker took his seat. Assistant District Attorney Dan Hiatt took the floor to cross-examine Tim Ketchum. He asked about Sandy's temper. Ketchum admitted that his little girl would hide knives in her bedroom "when she got upset."

The ADA then called Lieutenant Colonel Bruce Jordan to the stand, where he told the crowded, hushed courtroom how Holly had tried to escape upon capture (that was a stretch, since Holly had only tried to squirm out of the cuffs, and that could conceivably have been just an effort to make the restraints less painful).

Jordan told in some detail how the bodies had been found and of the numerous stab wounds that had been inflicted on the elderly couple. Jordan also claimed that the three missing knives from the Collier residence had been found in the stolen truck on Tybee Island.

When Jordan finished his testimony, Walker rose to his feet and pleaded that his client Sandy Ketchum was a juvenile and how "a lot of people have failed her." Concluding, he said, "We can't forget that they are children."

Judge English wasted no time. He quickly denied bond.

As the girls were led from the courtroom, a spectator on the Ketchum side yelled out, "We love you, Sandy!"

Tim Ketchum and Kevin Collier's paths crossed in the lobby of the courthouse. Both men embraced without saying a word.

As the distraught Ketchums emerged from the courthouse into the bright Georgia summer day, TV news crews descended upon them. With arms locked, they stoically walked on, ignoring the questions the reporters fired their way.

TWELVE

Pastor Glenn Stringham had been the first person to step inside the Collier house two days after the murders. Kevin Collier had opened the door for him. They were there to get clothes for Kevin's parents to be buried in.

Stringham had served in Vietnam as a Military Policeman. He was used to crime scenes, and had witnessed a lot of bloodshed, but he was taken aback by what he saw inside 226 Plantation Drive. Whole sections of carpet had been removed, but the blood had soaked through to the bare floors. Blood spatter covered the walls in the kitchen. What made it particularly painful for him was knowing that the blood belonged to his good friends, and how tragic a thing it was to happen to two precious people. It left Stringham with an empty feeling.

Kevin Collier wanted his dad buried in one of his Rush Limbaugh designer ties. His dad had loved Limbaugh and faithfully bought all his signature ties for his wardrobe. Stringham admired Limbaugh for his conservative views, but did not like his ties, calling them some of the ugliest ties he has ever seen. He and Kevin had a quiet laugh about his dad's correct political views but poor taste in neckties. Kevin picked one out, a Christmas theme one, and the two men quietly left the house.

The August 9 funeral for the Colliers was a combined church effort. First Baptist Church Atlanta brought a large contingent of their members down to the Fayetteville church. The choir and the famed orchestra would perform, with Kevin Collier playing the trombone.

The 1,000 mourners made too large a crowd for the stately church that stood in the center of town, so the service was held in the church's adjacent school gymnasium. Even the eighty-seat choir loft was full of people who had come to honor the Colliers. As Glenn Stringham surveyed the overflowing crowd, he was moved by all the good people from Atlanta, Fayetteville, and other local churches, friends from Delta, family from south Georgia, and even friends from Hawaii who'd made the effort to attend. Lieutenant Colonel Bruce Jordan and several of his detectives walked over from their county offices to take seats in the crowd. It was the first time Jordan had ever attended the funeral of a victim of a crime he was investigating.

The moving ceremony included sermons from three pastors of the two churches, who spoke in an upbeat way of the lives of Carl and Sarah Collier. Atlanta's Reverend John Glover drew knowing smiles from the audience when he spoke of Carl's conservative Republican beliefs and how the couple was now in the hands of God, smiling down on them all.

He told the assembled mourners not to blame God for the crimes that had occurred just days before:

"This is not God's fault. These girls used their moral freedom to step out of God's will. We are not promised tomorrow. Tell someone you love them."

Reverend Glover ended his eulogy by saying that the Colliers were not in their caskets, but were "already in Heaven."

Glenn Stringham addressed the caskets in front of him and, smiling, described the overflow crowd as just "a small gathering of your friends."

After recalling some of the good works of the Colliers, including Carl's mission in North Dakota, he speculated what may have been crossing the minds of the good Christian couple on the night of their murders: "I'm sure Sarah was thinking, 'Father, forgive them, for they know not what they do.'" A pall of thoughtful silence fell over the crowd.

Frank Ellis, the senior pastor at Fayetteville First Baptist Church, spoke of "the wicked plot to execute them" and wondered why the girls had made these incomprehensible decisions.

Five musical interludes were played by the full orchestra. TV crews from Atlanta filmed from outside, but were given a tape from inside that would be shown on the nightly news that evening and be picked up by other national outlets. Besides those of the local and Atlanta daily newspapers, *USA Today* and *People* magazine's reporters were in attendance.

Holly, age 3, feeds ducks on a camping trip with her grandparents.
Courtesy of Kevin Collier

A sad-looking Sandy, age 14,
on her way to a school dance.
Courtesy of the Ketchum Family

Holly, age 7, with her grandparents at a dance recital.
Courtesy of Kevin Collier

The Collier house—the murder scene.
Photo by Kevin F. McMurray

Kevin Collier in the Collier house next to the hallway that leads to Holly's bedroom.
Photo by Kevin F. McMurray

Exterior of the rear of the Collier house. The police could plainly see Sarah Collier's body at the foot of the basement stairs through the sliding glass door.
Photo by Kevin F. McMurray

Blood stains on the wall leading to Holly's room.
Courtesy of the Fayette County Sheriff's Department

Carl Collier's truck, stolen by Holly and Sandy after the murders and later found on Tybee Island.
Courtesy of the Fayette County Sheriff's Department

Lt. Colonel Bruce Jordan, lead investigator of the Colliers' murders, in his office.
Photo by Kevin F. McMurray

Aerial view of the Tybee Island beach house where Holly and Sandy were apprehended.
Courtesy of the Fayette County Sheriff's Department

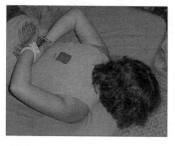

Holly handcuffed and lying face-down on a floor mattress moments after she was arrested.
Courtesy of the Fayette County Sheriff's Department

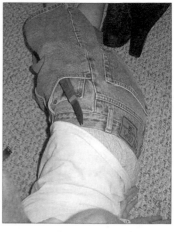

Sandy handcuffed on the floor on her arrest. Notice the knife in her pocket.
Courtesy of the Fayette County Sheriff's Department

Police display the two knives found in the truck that were later identified as the murder weapons.
Courtesy of the Fayette County Sheriff's Department

One of the murder weapons found in the stolen truck on Tybee Island.
Courtesy of the Fayette County Sheriff's Department

Sandy Ketchum's mug shot the day of her capture on Tybee Island.
Courtesy of the Fayette County Sheriff's Department

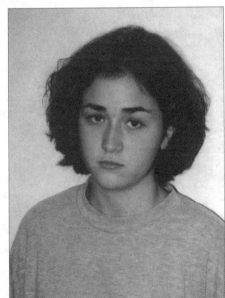

Holly Harvey's mug shot.
Courtesy of the Fayette County Sheriff's Department

The Fayette County Courthouse
Photo by Kevin F. McMurray

District Attorney Scott Ballard
Photo by Kevin F. McMurray

Lloyd Walker, Sandy Ketchum's lawyer
Photo by Kevin F. McMurray

Judy Chidester, Holly Harvey's lawyer
Photo by Kevin F. McMurray

Upon the completion of the service, the rousing hymn "How Great Thou Art" rang out in the cavernous gym. Kevin Collier played a small emotional solo on trombone. As the caskets were wheeled out, Widor's "Toccata" was played. The piece of music had special meaning to the Colliers' son. He had written of the moving wedding recessional in a message that appeared on the last page of the ceremony's flyer.

No one could have ever guessed my loving parents would have gone to the Lord this senseless way. I long to see them again . . . and have asked all the hard questions, but I know those answers are in God's hands.

Since the tragic and horrific events last Monday evening, you have poured out your love in amazing miraculous ways from unexpected places at unexpected times. In one way or another you have become my family now, and for that I am deeply grateful. Generous support coming from all directions shows God's faithfulness. My hope and desire is that your last memory of my parents today is that they are celebrating a new Holy Life together—free from the struggles here on earth. Today you are witnessing a joyous celebration honoring not only my parents' new heavenly lives, but also a demonstration of God's redeeming love by His people.

As you leave, Widor's "Toccata" will remind you of the wedding recessional when two are united in marriage. Today may this melody remind you that Mom & Dad are celebrating their new union with Christ together.

*Thank you so much for showing your sincere re-
spect by honoring my parents with your presence.*

Their legacy continues . . .

—Kevin Collier

On the back of the program it noted that, "Due to circumstances beyond our control, Carla Collier was not able to attend today's celebration."

Carla was in jail and had been refused permission by penal authorities to attend her parents' funeral, a funeral made necessary by actions of her daughter Holly.

More than a hundred mourners attended the graveside ceremony at the Westview Cemetery in Atlanta. It was brief, with reading of scriptures and the final blessings before the two caskets were lowered into the ground.

The Colliers were extended one last token of love and appreciation by their church. A veteran of many a funeral, Glenn Stringham knew Kevin Collier would have to come up with the $2,000 in cash for the grave-opening fee. Given the emotional crush he was experiencing, details such as this might have escaped him. Stringham had children of his own who were young adults, so he appreciated Kevin's predicament as a single person who worked long and hard and maintained his own home. He had called Kevin and asked if coming up with the fee would be a problem. Kevin admitted that, yes, it might. Stringham told him not to worry, and he would see to raising the money.

Stringham addressed the senior adult congregation exercise group that used the church school's gym on the Wednesday before the interment. He told them he wanted them to reach in their pockets to show Kevin how much his parents were loved, by helping him pay for the openings of the graves. Within the hour he had collected $1,600, and before the day was over the amount had grown to $2,600. It was a testament to the love and respect that the community had held for Carl and Sarah Collier.

THIRTEEN

District Attorney Scott Ballard says with a touch of pride that his great-great-great grandfather is buried in Fayette County, adding the obvious, "We've been here a long time." His roots in the legal community were also deep. His grandfather was a former sheriff of Fayette County and his father has, and continues to be, a practicing attorney there.

Ballard graduated from Fayetteville High School and the University of Georgia, and got his law degree from Florida State University in 1984. Entering private practice with his father, it took twenty years before he decided to enter politics in the spring of 2004. Scott Ballard believed that a change was needed in the Griffin Judicial Circuit, and decided to run for the office of district attorney.

Ballard saw that the DA's office was losing a lot of its cases. Things in the Fayette County Courthouse were chaotic. In March of 2004 there was a logjam of over 300 backed-up cases on the court trial calendar. Many of them were being dismissed before they could ever come to trial, and just five went before the bench. Of those five, three were mistrials, one was an acquittal. The acquittal was particularly galling.

The victim in the case couldn't identify the defendant as her assailant, a fact that hadn't been learned by District Attorney Bill McBroom's office until the victim was in the witness chair. Miscues like that had Scott Ballard concerned. Other than selfish ones, Ballard could not think of any reason not to run. He unseated the twenty-four-year veteran prosecutor handily in November of 2004.

Newly elected DA Ballard inherited the Collier murder case and was brought up to date by outgoing DA McBroom and Lieutenant Colonel Bruce Jordan. "Tragedy any way you look at it" is how Ballard describes the case.

"Part of it is tragic because the defendants are kids. Part of it is tragic because the victims' granddaughter is a suspect, and the manner of killing is horrifying. But I am chomping at the bit to try the case."

Scott Ballard's office had decided to try both 15-year-old Holly Harvey and 16-year-old Sandy Ketchum as adults. Ballard explains his belief by saying that the court system never envisioned such a horrific case ever being handled by the juvenile division. A case such as the Colliers' murders was beyond its ken and legal wherewithal.

Ballard recognizes that there are some mitigating factors in the teenage girls' lives that factored in, namely the fractured family life, drug and alcohol abuse, and neglect. But Ballard believes that all of these factors are "not nearly enough to overcome the aggravation of the act."

The white-haired district attorney would not comment on the strength of the case on legal grounds, but he would say he had "no hesitation trying this case anywhere," alluding to the fact that there was talk of getting a change of venue.

Ballard would personally try the case. Unlike most big city DAs, in less populous and rural counties of Georgia it is common for elected chief prosecutors to actually try cases themselves instead of delegating them to assistant district attorneys. With the fact that the murders were getting nationwide attention in the press (*USA Today, People* magazine, and Court TV to name a few), it could certainly be argued that publicity had some bearing on why the newly elected—and untested—DA decided to handle the case himself.

Ballard had never prosecuted a case, but the 45-year old rookie DA was "excited" and "looking forward" to trying this one personally. He believed having a fresh face and a gung-ho prosecutor might be better than a veteran ADA weary of the daily pressure of presenting a case before a hard-nosed trial judge. As Ballard said, with a smile and typical rural Southern aplomb, ". . . it's all fresh meat to me."

Trying the case in Fayette County, "the Pearl of Metropolitan Atlanta's Southern Crescent," presented some problems for the defense. It is a decidedly conservative, Republican county, many of whose citizens had flocked there in order to escape the rampant crime of urban Atlanta and some of its outlying counties. History and location did not bode well for the defense.

Fayette County was established by the state of

Georgia by resolution in 1821. The county was carved out of Creek Indian Territory and was named after one of General George Washington's lieutenants in the Revolutionary War, the Marquis De LaFayette. Fayetteville became the county seat in 1823. The old County Courthouse, erected in 1825, still stands proudly in the center of town after outliving its usefulness in 1985.

The county saw plenty of action during the Civil War, most of it cavalry fighting in what was to become known as The Battle of Atlanta. The sacking and burning of this important city by the Union's General William Tecumseh Sherman was a turning point of the war and was the inspiration of Margaret Mitchell's *Gone with the Wind*. The celebrated author of the best seller—and later blockbuster film—spent time in Fayette County researching her book. It seems that Mitchell's great-grandfather, Phillip Fitzgerald, was a landowner in the county in the 1830s, and he and his family later became the models for the O'Hara brood that resided in "Tara," the book's graceful antebellum plantation.

Fayette County is only 199 square miles, making it one of the smallest counties in the state, but it is one of the most affluent ones. Fayette County's proximity to Atlanta paid off as that city became one of the most dynamic and successful in the South. The establishment of Hartfield–Jackson Atlanta International Airport in 1925 on the city's southern outskirts spurred development of Fayette County to boom-time levels during the Cold War years.

The ambitious expansion of the airport in the 1950s also spawned a ring of industry and a vibrant economy.

An urgent need for workers swelled a population growth in the area. The newcomers spilled into Fayette County in search of suitable housing. The county was rural and pristine and it was also sparsely populated, easily accessible, and low in taxation.

A group of forward-thinking residents saw the potential problem of rampant unbridled development and put into place a thoughtful growth plan that recognized the eminent change from a rural to a suburban county. The building codes and regulations that were instituted were as enlightened as they were effective in preventing the urban sprawl of Atlanta from engulfing them. Such dogged pursuit of a quality of life was unheard of in the state of Georgia, particularly in underdeveloped counties such as Fayette. By the 1970s Fayette County had, in effect, become a bedroom community of Atlanta.

By the 1980s, with its astonishing growth rate, Fayette was viewed by most of the state as a county with safe neighborhoods, superior schools, (the highest SAT scores in the state), and quick, easy access to Atlanta. It was clean, conservative, and affluent. In the 1990s *American Demographics* magazine proclaimed Fayette as "America's Hottest County" and the venerable and conservative *Wall Street Journal* called it "one of the most attractive communities for corporate and family relocation."

Fayette, despite its huge shopping malls and other upper-middle-class suburban life trappings, prided itself in being firmly rooted in the traditions of the "Old South." Although conservative in its politics, the county is advanced in racial relations compared to

most of this area of the South. No doubt this is largely
due to the influx of minorities who worked at the airport and migrated south with white workers to find
homes. The American Dream seemed to be obtainable
in Fayette County. One of the best examples (some
might say ironic) was that the largest, most ostenta-
tious home in the county belonged to the African-
American former heavyweight boxing champion of the
world, Evander Holyfield. Holyfield's Tara-like man-
sion and separate guest house, full basketball court,
pool, and maintenance building is surrounded by 105
rolling acres of open fields and woods. The 15,000-
square-foot house, which boasts a gym, sauna, bowling
alley, and racquetball court, is a short drive from the
modest house at 226 Plantation Drive in nearby
Riverdale.

FOURTEEN

Kathleen M. Heide, PhD, is a Professor of Criminology at the University of South Florida in Tampa. She is one of the leading international experts on juvenile homicide and parricide. She is a psychotherapist and a frequent expert witness in homicide trials involving youths. In her career she has evaluated over a hundred kids who have killed. She is the author of *Why Kids Kill Parents* and *Young Killers*.

Heide, when evaluating cases like the murders of the Colliers, often sees a pattern where the kids have not had discipline or boundaries and rules set in place while growing up. Heide says this is a form of child abuse. Typically, in the cases of young killers who lived in undisciplined households during their formative years, when a suddenly aware parent, a new parent, a grandparent, or a guardian has tried to establish new rules, the juvenile has rebelled. Thankfully, the outcome rarely rates a headline.

According to Heide, good and effective parents will start to instill discipline in their children when they reach the ages of 2–5 years. For example, when a youngster wants something, perhaps a toy or an ice cream cone, and is told no, he may fly into a temper tantrum. The effective parent will not give in. Unfortunately, but understandably, a lot of parents, out of frustration or laziness, will cave in to the child's demands. As the child matures, this can develop into a serious problem, where the issues change but the pattern of the parenting discipline doesn't. These undisciplined children, says Heide, are not learning how to deal with frustration. They are not realizing that the world doesn't revolve around them and that sometimes in life you don't get what you want. Children have to learn to deal with that.

At ages 8–12 the stakes are higher. A turned-around parent, new parent, or authority figure walking into this situation may try to instill some semblance of order. At this time, the schools, neighbors, or the juvenile justice system might get involved, warning the guardian of the child that there may be a problem. Clinicians believe this is when therapy or intervention might be needed to help the child deal with frustration and unruliness.

At ages 12–17, when a parent or authority figure tries to instill discipline, the teenager will see this as someone who wants "to change the rules." The teenager in these cases has a level of personality development that is one of a much younger child. They have no sense of accountability for their behavior. When a kid has a lot of rage and is spiraling out of control, punishment is typically how it is dealt with. That, says Heide, is usually not the best solution. This is the scenario where cases of homicide can result—but Heide adds that there is no real way to predict it.

Typically there are only 1,000 to 1,500 cases a year (3,300 was the high point in 1994) where teenagers commit murder, arguably a low-base phenomenon. The best predictor of violence, says Heide, is other minor incidents of violence or the threat of violence. Heide relates that most authority figures and friends take such minor incidents as not serious and the threats as "just talk." These kids, according to Heide, need immediate clinical intervention.

Of the average high figure of 1,500 homicides committed by juveniles, fewer than 10 percent of them were perpetrated by girls, and of those, just a handful of the victims were a parent or a family member. When the female murderer does kill a parent or family member they often have accomplices or act in groups.

Heide has found that the female teenage murderers of a parent or guardian were frequently involved in gang activity, concealing a pregnancy, protecting a love interest, or having their activities interfered with by a parent.

Alcohol and drugs can also be an aggravating factor in any homicide. They can affect perception and inhibitions. Cocaine and methamphetamine use can have extremely onerous consequences. These two narcotics can cause acute agitation among users and, when coupled with anger, alienation, and low personality development, violent responses can be expected.

According to the 1996 National Household Survey of Drug Abuse, an ongoing and periodic examination of American drug habits in which the Center for Disease Control was a participant, those involved in homosexual activity were about three times more likely to be involved in illegal drug use.

Geoffrey McKee, a clinical professor in the department of neuropsychiatry at the University of South Carolina School of Medicine, says kids who grow up outside a stable environment are more likely to find their identity in relationships outside the family.

Lauren J. Woodhouse, a forensic psychologist in Toronto and the author of *Shooter in the Sky: The Inner World of Children Who Kill*, says that for girls, "the search for a new sense of belonging often begins as their sexuality kicks in—usually from age 12 to 16—when they're no longer the little dumpling." These types of girls who feel vulnerable and displaced don't often have a boyfriend and may bond with other girls—"disenfranchised girls, not yearbook girls." Woodhouse adds:

"With girls, it's not about ego [as with boys]. It's about belonging, about having a place to go and be. The relationship among a pair of girls or group of girls can be passionate. Within such a relationship, girls might do what they never would have done on their own. Among the girls a swarming mentality seemed to drive the crime."

Helen Smith, a forensic psychologist in Knoxville, Tennessee, says that many kids who kill are "narcissistic." Smith elaborates by saying: "Other people's lives mean nothing to them and they tend to go into a rage if somebody tries to put limits on them. One of them probably wouldn't have done anything, but get them together, with their distorted thinking, and that escalates into violence."

Smith relates that teenage girl patients of hers have told her that killing gave them "a sense of power" and that they say, "I could feel the person dying." For girls it is an "intimate act."

The choice of weapons by young killers is also telling. Multiple stabbings of victims, most experts agree, indicates a pattern of rage and disassociation. In a frenzied state there is a stress response or a kind of looping behavior where there is a loss of control. When a person is enraged there is a flood of emotion where the response becomes uncontrollable. Frenzied stabbing attacks suggest strong emotion: hatred and pent-up anger. Professor Heide says that in these cases the young murderers' mental competence certainly can be called into question.

A lack of remorse by dangerously anti-social juvenile offenders seems to indicate, again, developmental problems. The lack of good parenting can fail in laying a good foundation, notably in the child's empathy with other human beings. In effect they don't have a sense of guilt. Professor Heide says a good 40 percent of the killer kids whom she has evaluated do not have remorse for the murders they committed. Developmentally impaired, they see nothing they have done as being really wrong. The old terms for such delinquents were *psychopaths* or *sociopaths*. Today juvenile clinicians call this type of behavior *conduct disorder*.

"Dangerously anti-social teenagers," Heide related,

"slay, not because they are mentally ill or want to escape an abusive parent, but simply to remove an obstacle."

Remorse by the teen after the fact, says Heide, has to be suspect. Is it genuine? In a typical case, where the offending juvenile is incarcerated, what a therapist would want to do is find something to break through to these kids so that they take some accountability for what they have done and develop empathy for others.

Several years of residential and intensive therapy is often needed to help the kids make the attitude adjustment. The reality of the situation is that troubled youths don't get that treatment, even when ordered by a judge. Most correctional facilities simply don't have the resources.

Heide believes the public wants to hold immature kids to the same standard as adults. It is a now accepted scientific fact that the human brain does not fully mature until one reaches the age of about 25 years, and when a pattern of abuse or neglect is thrown into the mix, the maturation of the brain is further compromised. This is the crux of the problem: known scientific fact colliding with some of our foundations of legal accountability.

The legal accountability issue is based on concepts developed by English common law hundreds of years ago. According to common law, children under the age of 7 years were not accountable. Between the years of 7–14 there was a presumption that children lacked responsibility, which the state could argue otherwise. Over 14 the presumption was that children were responsible but the defense could argue otherwise and prevail. In 1899 in this country, juvenile laws were passed where special treatment and rehabilitation were substituted for jail time for kids in this last age bracket. But in the 1980s a more punitive treatment for teens came into vogue, where they were punished just like adults. It was an attitude of "If they're old enough to do the crime, they're old enough to do the time." In effect, society has regressed, claims Dr. Heide, in treating juvenile criminals, even though science has progressed to a point where we know criminally prone kids are not mature enough to be legally accountable.

Sandy and Holly were having a difficult time adjusting to prison life. Holly confided in her mother and her lawyer Judy Chidester that she was despairing. Sandy sent a steady stream of poems she had written to her parents. One of them, written on August 15, 2004, was particularly revealing.

"ENDING IT ALL"

Going down this road,
Watching the cars pass.
Feeling so much pain,
That corrupts from the past,

Thinking of what I've done,
Because it never goes away.
Jumping up to run,
From what happened that day.

Wanting to end it all,
I take a little spin.
Bashing my head into the wall,
Hoping death would begin.

Running so fast,
And bleeding so much.
Could I die at last?
And feel no touch.

Remembering the times,
When I was loved the most.
Feeling these rhymes,
And remembering the cost.

Finally laying to rest,
And saying a few good byes.
Knowing I tried my best,
To throw away the lies.

Sandy Ketchum

FIFTEEN

On November 24, Beth Ketchum received a revealing three-page letter in Sandy's neat script postmarked from Metro RYDC. The contents brought her to tears.

2: Moma Beth
4rm: Sandy VkV Deve
Date: November 24, 2004
Time: Mine
Place: Metro R4DC (my room)
Mood: Chillin. Frustrated. "Going nuts"!!
Mott: "Better to have something, then nothing at all"
Reason: Response to your letter
Request: w/b "ASAP"
Love: 100% always and forever
Hate: 0% never that
Song: Picture, Angel, I Miss You
Artist: Kid Rock, Amanda Perez, Aaliyah
Message: B.

E.

L.

O.

Wus happenin? Shidd just chillin in my room cuz we are in emergency count. They need to learn how to count 4 real, I mean it's not that hard. I'm glad you've written me. I just want you to know that I'm glad you and my dad are still together. If I didn't still have you standing tall by my side I would feel empty inside. I know you say you're not trying to take the place of my mom but you've had that place in my heart since we met. Sandra will never amount to what you mean to me, and when I say never I mean "NEVER". I know I'm gonna be locked up for a while but I want you to adopt me and become my other legal guardian. I mean I'm not gonna shut Sandra completely out of my life but you, my dad, and I deserve to have this (each other). I just wish I would've did things different. Even though I'm not physically there just think of me as if I were teddy or tessie laying in the bed next to you. I love you as the mom you are to me. There is no step to mother or daughter. I might of did things in the past that pissed you off real bad and make you think that I hated you but everytime you said you were gonna leave and left I always cried cause even though I knew you were gonna come back I didn't want to lose you over something childish that I did. I know there is nothing I can do to make up for the past 3 years of your life but at least now I can say "I'm sorry" and truly mean it from the bottom at my heart. I know I'm locked up but I'm starting over. I could've started over when I was locked up last year. But I knew deep down that I wasn't ready. That's why when I got out I went back to doing the same thing I was already doing. I guess it took something this tragic to show me that the life I was living wasn't kickin it. I believe I would be dead. From an overdose or a car crash, cuz Sandra and Kenny always let me drive the car, van, or truck whether they were with me or not and like I already told you we were always high even when ya'll came to see me. That's why I always told Daddy that I had just woke up. One of the main reasons I went to live with my mom was because she let me do the things that ya'll didn't, I was just sick of being told what to do, it didn't have anything to do with ya'll. And I also felt like it was time 4 me to see what my mom was like without daddy around. One thing that Sandra told me when she wrote me the other day was that the reason she let me do the things I did was because she didn't want to make me mad. Cuz she was like ya'll were with me when Everett [Everett McConnell, Sandy's half-brother by her mother's first marriage] lived with her. Everett felt like he got in trouble for dumb shit. Just like me. We really acted the same and we got into trouble 4 some well, really a lot of the same things. He poisoned Sandra, Kenny, Samantha, and James . . . and that's why he's locked up. He got 14 years do 7. Sandra told me that she felt as if she did it wrong by punishing Everett so she let me do what I wanted because she wanted me to be one of the only kids she could actually keep. Don't get me wrong cuz I do miss her a lot. I might not of lived with her for a long time but out of the time I was there we went through alot. Her and Kenny used to lit-

erally fist fight all the time. I seen Sandra get beat to hell and back and then Kenny get beat to hell and back. They used to have seizures all the time. That's part of the reason I used to go to Holly's house every weekend, so I wouldn't have to deal with them fighting and shit. But even when I did go to Holly's I had to deal with her and her grandparents arguing. This is why I told Holly that I couldn't take it no more (going to her house every weekend and hiding from her grandparents). So, I was getting myself together to leave but she didn't want me to leave. And then this happened. But anywayz . . . I didn't mean to get side tracked like that. How have ya'll been doing? Hopefully good. I miss ya'll so much. Well, let me go.

Love you,
Sandy

PS. W/b ASAP

SIXTEEN

The meeting in a conference room at the Fayette County Courthouse was scheduled for Thursday, March 24, 2005. Present were Griffin Judicial Circuit Judge Paschal English Jr., Judge Johnnie Caldwell, DA Scott Ballard, lawyers for the two defendants, Lloyd Walker and Judy Chidester, a clerk, and a court reporter. Holly Harvey and Sandy Ketchum were not present. Trial motion dates, trial dates, and trial locations were to be discussed.

Judge Paschal English was a well-known figure in the state of Georgia if not the nation. His notoriety was due not so much to his judicial work, but to his iconic image in American pop culture. Paschal English had had the envied status of being a selected contestant on the hugely popular CBS TV show *Survivor: Marquesas*, which aired to record-breaking audiences back in February 2002.

English's participation on the program was a well-kept secret in the Griffin Judicial Circuit, but speculation was rampant as to his whereabouts. Unbeknownst to all but family and a few close friends, English was on the remote island in the South Pacific building his own shelter and foraging for food and water in competition with others who had their eyes on the $1 million top prize money. English was a fit athlete and a retired colonel in the US Air Force, having served a stint in the Vietnam War from 1971–72. He kept in shape with a rigorous running routine and is a familiar figure dashing about the streets of his home town of Thomaston, Georgia.

English finished in fourth place on the show, which was filmed from November to December 2001. On the program he was affectionately known as "Pappy," and never received the dreaded elimination vote from his peers. According to the program producers he was one of the most popular figures, to fellow contestants and to the viewing audience, ever to compete on the show. English, however, was eliminated from contention on the reality show when he drew the "purple rock."

A graduate of the University of Georgia in Athens, with a doctorate degree in Jurisprudence and a former chief assistant district attorney for twelve years, Judge English, a faithful husband of thirty-five years and father of two grown children, was also no stranger to high-profile and news-making cases in the Griffin Judicial Circuit.

One of those cases dealt with the most famous citizen of Fayette County, former heavyweight boxing champion of the world Evander Holyfield. In 1998 a paternity suit was filed against him that got wide publicity in the print and broadcast media—no doubt due to the insatiable appetite the American public has for information on the sexual proclivities of the rich and famous.

English also sat on the bench for the worst multiple murder case in Fayette County history. Isaac Jerry Pearson, 66 years of age, was charged with killing Donnie Gee, Barbara Clark, 16-year old Nikki Underwood, and 3-year old Doeyanna Burton on December 28, 1999. English accepted Pearson's guilty plea in exchange for a life sentence without parole.

Yet English was certainly no liberal-leaning judge, as another case in 1999 proved. Judge English denied a request for appeal by a 19-year-old who was cited for a traffic violation for underage possession of alcohol. The teenager's lawyer had argued that his client was not doing anything that had to do with traffic! English's refusal to grant the appeal, and the guilty verdict itself, were overturned by the Court of Appeals of Georgia.

Showing an apparent lack of tolerance for traffic violators, English prevented a planned concert that was to benefit the charitable organization Habitat for Humanity. It seems the well-known do-good organization had failed to note that the Senoia Raceway, where the benefit was scheduled to be held, was not zoned for concerts, and the expected hordes of people would cause traffic, sanitation, and security problems. Habitat for Humanity's failure to follow the letter of the law cost the charity an estimated $100,000 after canceling the show.

Despite his presiding over heinous crime trials and other cases of legal note, Paschal English is probably most famous for his involvement in the so-called "booty dancing" case. English had shut down a teen club called the Market in the summer of 2000 after prosecutors showed the judge a tape, secretly taken by undercover sheriff's department detectives, of the "booty dancing" being done by teens there. Booty dancing involved females grinding their pelvic areas with the groins of their male partners. It was deemed by English as "promoting sex under the excuse of dancing." English found it so offensive that not only was the club ordered shut, but the owners were charged with contributing to the delinquency of minors.

Defense lawyers objected and claimed the conservative jurist was biased against rap music. Judge English was quoted in an Associated Press article saying, "They could have been dancing to 'Jesus Loves Me.' I don't care what they are doing in New York, San Francisco, Atlanta, or anywhere else in the country."

Judge English ran unopposed in the last election, getting 100 percent of the vote in the conservative counties he served.

One of the trial venues offered by the DA's office was on St. Simons Island, city of Brunswick, Glynn County. Walker and Chidester did not like the location, believing it was too close to Tybee Island where the girls had been captured. Even though Brunswick got most of its TV news from Jacksonville, Florida (the defense's objective was to get a venue which got most of its TV news outside of Georgia), the case had gotten a lot of attention in the Savannah media and was deemed too prejudicial to a potential jury in nearby Glynn County. The other locale was Thomasville,

Thomas County, in southern Georgia, whose main source of news came out of nearby Tallahassee, Florida. It was quickly agreed by the defense and prosecution that the small remote town would be where the trials would be held.

DA Scott Ballard was concerned that the defense could still use the pre-trial publicity issue even after a change of venue had been agreed on. He was afraid the Thomasville public would start getting bombarded by the local media once it was announced that the trial would be held there, and the defense team would leap on that. The trial judges would file the change of venue on May 13 and schedule a hearing on pre-trial motions on Tuesday, April 26.

The logistics of holding the trials in Thomasville also worried Ballard. There was talk of conducting both trials simultaneously in the same small courthouse, but that might have proved unwieldy, what with witnesses and investigating police officers shuttling back and forth. There was also the everyday business of the Thomas County court system that would have to be accommodated. Ballard admitted he may have needed "a choreographer to pull it off."

The most likely scenario was to hold the trials back to back, allotting one week for each. But what if the first case ran too long? Would trial reports in the media prejudice the second? Should they sequester both juries?

The mundane details also had bothered him. Would everybody involved be able to get accommodations in proximity to the courthouse, and would the extended stays in distant Thomasville cause hardship? Ballard had already made a decision in his mind about a plea deal.

Ballard had always been confident he would get a conviction if the case went before a jury, because the evidence against the girls was strong. He knew, of course, that it was never a "sure thing" when the guilt or innocence of a defendant was in the hands of twelve honest and impartial people. All it took was one juror to hold out. The former defense attorney and newly elected DA was eager to prove himself, but in the end he felt the plea bargains were fair to the defendants and to the interests of the good people of Georgia.

At this time the defense attorneys had not yet received "discovery evidence" from the DA's office. Discovery evidence included crime-scene photos, murder weapon photos, taped interviews with suspects, and other evidence pertinent to the prosecution's case that they were bound by law to share with the defense.

The discovery evidence law had only been on the books for a few years. Prior to that, a defendant would often go to trial not knowing how strong a case the prosecution had against them, or in legal slang, "trial by ambush." By legal standards, discovery evidence leveled the playing field.

Walker and Chidester had a pretty good idea what was in the discovery evidence, but they had not seen it yet. The defense's strategy at that time was to test the legality of evidence the prosecution was going to present. They had no real hope of suppressing a lot of it, but due to the tenor and seriousness of the charges, they felt obliged to try to test some of it. Walker had some issues with statements Sandy Ketchum may have made after her arrest, but he knew the physical evidence would be hard to refute. There were also the statements made by prosecution witness Sara Polk about Holly and Sandy's visit to her house, covered in blood, brandishing knives, and boasting about the murders that would be hard to exclude from being heard by a jury.

The defense teams didn't know it at the time, but the forensic evidence was indeed damning. On August 24, 2004, the Georgia Bureau of Investigation (GBI) Division of Forensic Sciences in Atlanta had received sealed packages from the Fayette County Sheriff's Office containing the kitchen knives and two pairs of blue jeans, all found in Carl Collier's truck on Tybee Island. Then on January 28, 2005, the lab received yet another sealed package containing three tubes of blood taken from Holly Harvey and three from Sandy Ketchum, in accordance with an approved search warrant. GBI also received blood samples from Carl and Sarah Collier.

On March 15, Forensic Biologist Diana Williams had concluded with "reasonable certainty" that the DNA obtained from one knife and one of the pairs of jeans belonging to Sandy matched the blood sample belonging to Sarah Collier. The DNA profiles from the second knife matched Sarah's and Carl Collier. The DNA profile from the second pair of jeans was inconclusive.

Since all the crime-scene items had been taken and tested in accordance with approved procedures, and the suspects' blood samples legally obtained, the defense teams had little hope of getting DNA results thrown out as inadmissible evidence. Scientifically, at least, conviction of both girls looked like a slam dunk for the prosecution.

Judge English then asked the lawyers if any plea offers had been made. Chidester and Walker had not solicited any offers from the DA, since they had not yet felt comfortable with the case or seen the discovery evidence. DA Ballard then made a surprising statement. He informed the judges and defense counsel that his office was prepared to offer pleas of two murders with malice that would carry two life sentences to run consecutively for Holly Harvey and two felony murder charges carrying two life sentences to run concurrently for Sandy Ketchum.

Murder with malice by Georgia law is when you intentionally kill someone. Felony murder is less serious. It is when, in the commission of a felony that is inherently dangerous, someone unintentionally gets killed. A good example of this would be if three felons conspire to rob a convenience store and one stays in the car and two go inside, one armed with a gun. The convenience store clerk is shot dead. Georgia law says both felons who had not actually killed anyone can be charged with felony murder.

Sandy had been facing two counts of murder with malice and one count of armed robbery. Under the statutory mandated sentencing rules, that meant that, if convicted on all charges and getting the maximum sentences, Sandy was looking at spending a total of 42 years behind bars before being considered for parole. The Georgia State Board of Pardons and Paroles, part of the executive branch of the state, were not statutorily required by law to adhere to those guidelines, and could either add or reduce time served—that was up to their "discretionary decision." Sandy, according to the guidelines, would have to serve only 14 years before being eligible for parole.

If Holly accepted her deal she would have to serve a minimum of 10 years for each charge, meaning a total minimum of 20 years before parole could be considered.

The conference ended after just a half hour. Both defense lawyers left knowing some big decisions would have to be made by their clients—and soon.

Lloyd Walker spoke to DA Ballard afterwards in private. Since Sandy had cooperated immediately upon her arrest on Tybee Island, and had confessed in full and was willing to cooperate with the prosecution in testimony against Holly at trial, Walker needed to know if the deal would still be on the table if Holly accepted her plea bargain and didn't go to trial, thereby negating the need for Sandy's cooperation. Ballard assured Walker that the plea arrangement would be good at least until Friday, April 1, eight days away. If Walker accepted the plea bargain on his client's behalf before that "drop dead" date, Ballard would honor it no matter what Holly Harvey decided to do.

Lloyd Walker knew he had to move fast on this to serve the best interests of Sandy Ketchum. He knew both judges were strict, and there would be no room for defense motions to soften the plea bargain. Neither Judge English nor Judge Caldwell had commented on the deal spelled out by Ballard. To Walker that meant they had no objections to it, which was "significant," but if the deal wasn't struck soon they could change their minds. The trial judges, ultimately, would have to approve of the deal. Walker also learned that Kevin Collier, son of the victims, and "people with the greatest interest in the case" (family and friends), had approved of the plea deal when they were apprised of it by the DA.

Walker went home that afternoon and gave the plea arrangement a great deal of thought. On Tuesday, following the proceedings, he informed Sandy's parents of the deal on the table, then quickly arranged a consultation with Sandy at the Metro RYDC where she was imprisoned. Walker had received reports that Sandy was depressed and not coping well with the reality of life in jail. He called Dr. Nancy Aldridge, Sandy's prison psychiatrist, and asked whether Sandy was competent to make a rational decision dealing with her fate. Aldridge reported that she was depressed but otherwise "okay."

Sandy Ketchum was about to make the second biggest decision of her life. The first, of course, was when she decided to take part in the murder of the Colliers.

On Tuesday, March 29, attorney Lloyd Walker met with Sandy Ketchum and her parents at Metro and informed her that the time had come to make the hard decision. She could discuss it with her parents, but in the end it would have to be her choice.

Walker still had not seen the discovery evidence, but he proceeded to explain the plea bargain deal: what the evidence would probably show, what she could expect if she took her chances with a trial, and the probable outcome if she lost in court. If she accepted the deal, and Holly did not accept hers, she would have to testify against Holly and would have to cooperate fully with the prosecution case against her lover. There would also be questions about her role in the murders which she would have to answer. Specifically, Walker explained, she would have to truthfully tell who stabbed whom, and when, and with what knife, all in open court. Essentially she would have to "roll over" on Holly. Sandy, said Walker, was "okay with all of that." Walker gave Sandy a day to think it over.

From her defense's point of view, Sandy was in this ugly situation because of Holly Harvey. Despite any residual feelings she may have for Holly, Walker told her, "It was time to take care of Sandy." Sandy agreed.

Sandy was willing to own up to what had happened and accept the consequences. She knew her actions the night of August 2, 2004, were horrible, but she didn't want to go to prison for 42 years and totally lose her life. Walker told her he thought it was an "extraordinarily good deal for her, all things considered." The plea deal gave her a chance to salvage something of her life after 14 years in prison. Sandy would only be 30 years old when she would emerge from behind bars. Marriage, motherhood, a career would still be possible.

Walker believed "this lesbian thing" was more a product of teenage infatuation, although, he admitted, there was a genuine emotional attachment between the two girls. The salaciousness of the homosexual relationship between Holly and Sandy was never particularly compelling to Walker. It was, according to him, more a result of the media playing on the "sexiness" of the case to appeal to the prurient interest of its TV audience and newspaper readership.

Back at Metro on Wednesday, March 30, Sandy Ketchum gave her lawyer the okay to accept DA Ballard's offer.

Walker returned home and drafted a letter, which he admitted was half-written anyway, to DA Ballard accepting the plea bargain, and faxed it to him that afternoon, hours before the DA's deadline. He followed up with a note to Ballard asking for assurances that Judge Johnnie Caldwell would sign off on the deal. Walker also advised Holly's attorney, Judy Chidester, of their intentions.

On Thursday, Lloyd Walker received the discovery evidence. Crime-scene photos, police reports, medical examiner reports, and DNA evidence made up the voluminous file. Walker found no "time bomb" to cause him to back out of the plea bargain. It was pretty much what he'd expected.

On Wednesday morning Judy Chidester received a call from Judge Paschal English's office inquiring if she and her client could be at the courthouse at 11 AM the next day so that they could get "this thing done under the radar." Despite his notoriety as a *Survivor* contestant and his apparent affinity for the camera, Judge English did not want to turn his courtroom into a media circus. Chidester agreed.

To her surprise the courthouse was crawling with members of the press and TV crews down from Atlanta. Chidester asked several of them how they had found out about the hurriedly scheduled hearing. To a man, they replied, "Bruce Jordan."

Chidester had been "stunned" as to the amount of information Bruce Jordan had released to the press. She claimed that the media people she had spoken to told her that they couldn't recall a case where so much information had been released to them by the lead investigator. This had her concerned about the ability to get a fair trial for Holly.

Jordan said that the girls had no defense, and any jury that would see the crime-scene photos would come to the same conclusion, and have no sympathy for them. The defense lawyers, according to Jordan, attacked the sheriff's department because they had no defense. But, said Jordan, if the defense didn't want the information released, they should have waived all pretrial hearings where all information becomes public record available to anyone, including the media.

Jordan could only shake his head in resignation when accused of being a showboater. His camera-friendly reputation was, no doubt, due to the fact that in the past, Sheriff Johnson had ordered that only the media-savvy Jordan would represent his office to the press.

Because of his involvement in solving high-profile cases like the Flint River murders, and now the Collier murders, and the subsequent media attention, a lot of people believed that Bruce Jordan had an agenda. There were some rumblings about him running for sheriff when the long-sitting Randall Johnson stepped down. Jordan would admit that the office might interest him if it were to be vacated. But according to him, his main goal was to clear all homicides that had been committed on his and his sheriff's watch. The glare of the media was beyond his control.

The Fayette County Sheriff's Office soon thereafter got a scathing review by the local paper *The Citizen News*. They were particularly lambasted for poor reporting to the local papers and for falling over themselves in getting their faces on the glamorous national and Atlanta TV news programs. In a letter to the editor, Bruce Jordan wrote that it was a matter of the well-funded and amply-staffed TV news people "paying attention to us" rather than the other way around.

On the flip-side of the media flap, Jordan wrote: "Lawyers and their clients complain that I talk to the media too much; the media and my wife complain that I don't talk to them enough."

The information released on the Collier case was something beyond the control of Jordan. The facts related to the case that were being scrutinized by the press were a result of the defense asking for the hearings. The media were always present for court appearances in sensational cases and, of course, it was all public record. It was their fault that so much was out there, not the DA's or sheriff's offices.

Jordan thought it was "funny" that he was accused of showboating when he appeared on the same news reports as the defense lawyers. Jordan admitted that such accusations used to bother him, but not anymore. Jordan loves what he does, and if working hard brought him all this "bull," he could live with it.

◆ ◆ ◆

When the voluminous discovery evidence package arrived, Judy Chidester quickly opened it. Notable among it all were the photos of the murders: four hundred in all. They were the most disturbing crime-scene photos she had ever seen in her long career as an attorney for the defense. She immediately knew it was important that Holly see them: that would help to hammer home what she had done and what a jury and her family would see. Chidester selected the most graphic and took them with her when she visited Holly at the Clayton County RYDC over in Lovejoy.

When Holly looked at the pictures she became, according to Chidester, "extremely distraught." One of the close-up photos showed her granddad lying face down in a pool of blood which grotesquely reflected his wide-eyed death grimace. Another showed her grandma hideously sprawled face up at the bottom of the cellar staircase, framed in a sea of crimson. As much as she hated to do it, Chidester felt compelled to show Holly what she would be confronted with in the event of a trial. She asked Holly what she would think upon viewing these photos of carnage if she were a jury member. Holly shook in uncontrollable fits and uttered, "No, no, no."

Chidester told Holly to think over all that she had told her and also asked permission to apprise her mom of developments. Holly agreed, but told her lawyer she didn't want to speak with her mother.

The next day, in a phone conversation with Chidester, Holly agreed to take the plea deal offered by

Scott Ballard. She asked for assurance that if she had no jury, the public, and most important, her family, would never see the horrible crime-scene photos. Judy Chidester assured her no one would.

It was clear to Judy Chidester from the very beginning that the prosecution had a strong case against her client. Complicating matters was the mental state of Holly Harvey since her capture seven months earlier. According to Chidester, Holly had spent much of her time in prison distraught, depressed, and under continual suicide watch. It took several visits for Holly to grow comfortable with Chidester and for her to help in her defense. Holly continually asked if her mother and Uncle Kevin hated her. She also wanted to know where Sandy was, and if was she all right. In their conferences Holly would get visibly upset and cry, and often get hysterical. Chidester grew so concerned about the effects her meetings with Holly had that she felt compelled to alert prison authorities to watch her carefully, telling them that Holly was "looking at two counts of malice murder and armed robbery, and who wouldn't be upset about that?"

Holly had a long time to think about how severe the consequences would be for what she had done. She had "significant problems" understanding the legal issues swirling around her. Chidester had only to remember what Holly reportedly had said upon her capture and arrest on Tybee Island: "Are my grandparents all the way dead?"

There were also times when Holly would ask if she would be home before school started.

Once the disturbed 16-year-old grasped the seriousness of the charges against her, Chidester had to reas-
sure her over and over that she would not be facing the
death penalty because of her age. Likewise she could
not be sentenced to life without the chance of parole.
But Chidester was careful and realistic with her client.
She didn't want Holly misinterpreting her. Chidester
didn't see it as her job to tell clients what they wanted
to hear. The job required brutal honesty—but she knew
she had to apply it differently when her client was just
a teenager.

Judy Chidester was also concerned that if Holly refused the plea bargain, there might not be enough time
to sift through the mountains of evidence to decide
whether pre-trial motions would be relevant. There
was so little time left.

Lloyd Walker and Judy Chidester had a working
agreement to combine resources to pursue common
goals together, such as the venue change and challeng-
ing the state about the amount of information being released. The two friends had several strategy sessions,
but they knew there would come a time when their interests would diverge and they would have to quit cooperating with each other. With the week leading up to
the April 7 hearing, that time had come.

One of the things Judy Chidester wanted explained
to Holly was why Sandy Ketchum's deal was significantly more lenient than hers. Ballard told her, based
on what Bruce Jordan had told him, that it was because
of Sandy's cooperation with the investigating police.
Chidester believed her client was unfairly being described in the media as cold-hearted, without remorse,

a stone-cold killer, and evil, because that was what
Bruce Jordan was telling them. She didn't find that to
be the case at all. Holly was indeed remorseful and had
been torn apart by her murderous actions, which she
could not explain. Chidester believed that because
Sandy had cooperated immediately, she had been la-
beled as remorseful. Chidester explained that people
react differently dealing with guilt. Holly had simply
shut down, and had been in denial in dealing with
events of August 2.

Both defense lawyers believed that alone, neither
girl would have been capable of committing the murders. Chidester was never sure if Holly had been the
ringleader, as portrayed in the press.

Chidester knew that drug use would not be a mitigating factor. Holly was on prescribed drugs for depression and she had information that showed that,
while in the care of Connie Earwood in the weeks prior
to the murders, the medication had ceased. By Georgia
law, terminating prescribed medication, either voluntarily or non-voluntarily, was no excuse for murder.
Likewise illegal drug use, specifically smoking crack
the day of the murders, was not a legally viable defense. However, Chidester and Walker both believed
the crimes would never have been committed had the
girls not been impaired by drugs. Chidester knew she
could only have brought up the drug issues in the hopes
of getting a lighter sentence after a conviction at trial.
She hoped it would not come to that.

The willingness of the defendants to accept the plea
deal was communicated by the DA's office to Judge

English on the afternoon of Wednesday, April 13. English's response was, "Hell, let's do this tomorrow."

That same day Walker was advised by Judy Chidester that Holly would be accepting her plea. Walker quickly called the DA's office, wanting assurances that Sandy's plea deal was still on the table. Walker believed, despite the DA's promises, that they "weren't out of the woods yet." Walker suspected Judges English and Caldwell were not entirely comfortable with the arrangements, and could nix any deal if "something" popped up at Holly's allocution. Would Holly answer all questions forthrightly to Judge English's satisfaction? Would she get sassy and aggravate him? Would her demeanor be appropriate? Would she show regret? Judge English had the power to throw out the plea bargain if he didn't like what he heard. Lloyd Walker worried about such things as he walked into one of the oak-paneled courtrooms of the Fayette County Courthouse at 10 AM Thursday, April 7.

Walker had Sandy's parents bring some nice clothes for her to wear at the hearing, not wanting her to appear in front of the judge and the unavoidable cameras in prison togs.

Judge Caldwell arrived at the courthouse before the 11 AM hearing. The sheriff's office had had their hands full arranging the transport of the prisoners in the high-profile case, as well as those involved in another case being adjudicated that day at the courthouse. Judge English and Walker were left to twiddle their thumbs until Sandy was brought in. No one had informed Judge Caldwell of the delays and it was obvious he was growing annoyed. Lloyd Walker recalls that

Caldwell started "fussing" to him. Walker remembers thinking, "I don't need this."

Walker excused himself and walked over to the courtroom next door, where Holly's hearing was just getting under way. Walker took a seat in the front row of the gallery. Tim and Beth Ketchum, Carla (who had been released from prison in September 2004) and Kevin Collier were also there, along with the media. The TV stations from Atlanta had pooled resources. One camera was set up to videotape the entire proceeds.

The impending drama was almost palpable. Walker sat apprehensively in the straight-backed wooden chair. His hands were sweating and his collar seemed unusually tight. He knew it was his nerves conspiring against him. He tried to focus on what should go right and not wrong yet Lloyd Walker knew that the fate of his client was linked to how Holly comported herself and if her answers to Judge English's questions were honest and contrite. Walker shifted his ample bulk in the chair and stared to his right at the door through which the defendant Holly Harvey would be making her entrance.

SEVENTEEN

Holly Harvey was led manacled into the courtroom and took her seat at the defense table to the right of the bench. She was neatly dressed in a pink business suit that Carla had provided to deputies while her daughter was in a holding cell.

The dour-faced Judge Paschal English shuffled through some papers before speaking.

THE COURT: Ms. Chidester, good morning.

MS. CHIDESTER: Good morning.

THE COURT: How you doing?

MS. CHIDESTER: Your Honor, Ms. Calloway was the guardian in this case.

THE COURT: I'm sorry?

MS. CHIDESTER: Ms. Calloway was the guardian in this case, which is why I have her sitting with me.

THE COURT: Fine. Thank you. I figured that's why she was sitting there. Thank you. All right. Mr. Ballard, if you're ready, sir.

MR. BALLARD: We are, Your Honor.

THE COURT: Do you want to bring her in, please? Miss Harvey.

(Pause in proceedings.)

MR. BALLARD: Okay. Miss Holly Harvey, would you come forward, please, with your attorney?

(Defendant and counsel approach the bench.)

DA Scott Ballard got up from his seat from behind the prosecution table and walked to a spot in front of the bench with a sheaf of papers in his hand. Judge English nodded in the DA's direction. That was Ballard's cue. The courtroom became deathly still. Ballard rocked on his heels as he spoke.

MR. BALLARD: Is your correct name Holly Harvey?
THE DEFENDANT: Yes, sir.
MR. BALLARD: Would you tell us what your date of birth is, Ms. Harvey?
THE DEFENDANT: March twenty-third of 89.
THE COURT: Speak up, please.
THE DEFENDANT: March twenty-third, 1989.
MR. BALLARD: And you're represented by Ms. Judy Chidester, is that correct?
THE DEFENDANT: Yes, sir.
MR. BALLARD: Has she represented you as well as you would like for her to during this matter?
THE DEFENDANT: Yes, sir.
MR. BALLARD: Has she explained to you the charges against you?

THE DEFENDANT: Yes, sir.

MR. BALLARD: Has she discussed with you any potential defenses that you may have?

THE DEFENDANT: Yes, sir.

MR. BALLARD: Are you satisfied with her diligence in representing you and in her advice to you up to this point?

THE DEFENDANT: Yes, sir.

MR. BALLARD: Do you understand that you've been charged with, for purposes of standing here today, two counts of malice murder; that the range of punishment on each of those counts is a life sentence? You understand that?

THE DEFENDANT: Yes, sir.

MR. BALLARD: You understand what you're charged with and the range of punishment, is that correct?

THE DEFENDANT: Yes, sir.

DA Ballard spoke in a monotone and only looked at Holly when he finished his prepared questions. Holly's answers, in her decidedly street tone, were barely audible to the gallery, who were craning their necks to hear.

MR. BALLARD: Your Honor, if the court—if we were to go to trial, we would show that on August the second—second, 2004, Miss Harvey, acting in conjunction with Miss Sandra Ketchum, killed with a knife by stabbing numerous times Holly Harvey's grandparents, Carl Collier and Sarah—Sarah Collier; that they then took the vehicle that the Colliers owned by force and took it with them to—to the coast of Georgia, where they were apprehended later and charged with these offenses. I need to notify you of some rights, Miss Harvey [. What] we're trying to do is to make sure that you're freely and voluntarily entering your plea today. Okay? And I need you to answer out loud to me so the court reporter can hear what you say and so that the judge can hear what you say. Okay?

THE DEFENDANT: Yes, sir.

MR. BALLARD: All right. Do you understand the nature of the offenses that you're charged with?

THE DEFENDANT: Yes, sir.

MR. BALLARD: Do you understand that by entering a plea of guilty, you waive the right to a trial by jury and the right to counsel at that trial?

THE DEFENDANT: Yes, sir.

MR. BALLARD: Do you understand that by entering a plea of guilty, you waive the right to the presumption of innocence?

THE DEFENDANT: Yes, sir.

MR. BALLARD: Do you understand that by entering this plea of guilty you waive the right to confront witnesses against yourself?

THE DEFENDANT: Yes, sir.

MR. BALLARD: Do you understand that by entering this plea of guilty you waive the right to subpoena witnesses?

THE DEFENDANT: Yes, sir.

MR. BALLARD: Do you understand that by entering this plea of guilty you waive the right to testify and to offer other—other evidence other than testimony?

THE DEFENDANT: Yes, sir.

MR. BALLARD: Do you understand that if you went to trial you would have the right not to incriminate yourself and that by pleading not guilty or remaining silent and not entering a plea, one obtains a jury trial, but by entering this plea, you're waiving that right?

THE DEFENDANT: Yes, sir.

MR. BALLARD: And do you further understand the terms of any negotiated plea that we've entered?

THE DEFENDANT: Yes, sir.

MR. BALLARD: Do you understand that a recommendation, if any, made by the state may be accepted or rejected by the court?

THE DEFENDANT: Yes, sir.

MR. BALLARD: Do you understand the maximum possible sentence on the charges, including that possible from consecutive sentences and enhanced sentences where provided by law?

THE DEFENDANT: Yes, sir.

MR. BALLARD: Do you understand the mandatory minimum sentence, if any, on this charge?

THE DEFENDANT: Yes, sir.

MR. BALLARD: You—you are a citizen of the United States, is that correct?

THE DEFENDANT: Yes, sir.

MR. BALLARD: Are you under the influence of alcohol or drugs at the present time, so that you don't understand what's going on here today?

THE DEFENDANT: No, sir.

THE COURT: Thank you, Mr. Ballard.

MR. BALLARD: Yes, sir.

THE COURT: Anything you're wanting to say, Mr. Ballard?

MR. BALLARD: No, Your Honor. We'd ask you to accept our recommendation.

THE COURT: Ms. Chidester, anything you're wanting to say, or Miss Harvey?

MS. CHIDESTER: Your Honor, Miss Harvey asked me to make a few comments on her behalf.

First, I'd like to say that this case for—for me has been prof—personally and professionally very difficult because of the nature of the crime and because of the fact that my client was fifteen years old. That's made it—That's made it difficult. There have been a good number of people that have come forward, people that knew her from church, people that knew her from school, that have come through me to offer their support and prayers for Miss Harvey, and I've given her all those messages, and she wants to express her gratitude for the people who have offered to keep her in their thoughts and prayers. She has asked me to express her deep remorse over her actions. It's something that she says she can only hope that one day she will forgive herself so that then she might ask others to attempt to forgive her.

We would ask that the court accept this plea that's been negotiated with the state and enter it accordingly.

Thank you.

THE COURT: Miss Harvey, how old are you right now?

THE DEFENDANT: Sixteen.

THE COURT: Speak up.

THE DEFENDANT: Sixteen.

THE COURT: Sixteen?

THE DEFENDANT: Yes, sir.

THE COURT: First of all, I want to make a finding for the record that, based on the questions that were asked to you, I find that you are freely and voluntarily entering your plea of guilty to the charges of malice murder—two counts of malice murder.

THE DEFENDANT: Yes, sir.

THE COURT: I'll also accept the factual basis that Mr. Ballard presented in support of these pleas.

Now, the persons or people you killed were who?

THE DEFENDANT: My grandparents.

THE COURT: And what were their names?

THE DEFENDANT: Carl and Sarah Collier.

THE COURT: How old were they?

THE DEFENDANT: Their seventies. I'm not sure.

THE COURT: In their seventies?

THE DEFENDANT: Yes, sir.

THE COURT: Were you living with them at the time?

THE DEFENDANT: Yes, sir.

THE COURT: Why were you living with your grandparents?

THE DEFENDANT: My mother was incarcerated.

THE COURT: For what?

THE DEFENDANT: Possession of marijuana.

THE COURT: How long had you lived with your grandparents?

THE DEFENDANT: They raised me all my life.

THE COURT: So for fifteen years you lived with your grandparents?

THE DEFENDANT: On and off.

THE COURT: Mostly on?

THE DEFENDANT: No, sir.

THE COURT: Well, you said on and off. Did you live with your mother more than you did your grandparents?

THE DEFENDANT: Yes, sir.

THE COURT: But your grandparents were central figures in your life, were they not?

THE DEFENDANT: Yes, sir.

THE COURT: The young lady that assisted you or participated in this crime with you, her name was what?

THE DEFENDANT: Sandy Ketchum.

THE COURT: And how old was Sandy at the time this happened?

THE DEFENDANT: Sixteen.

THE COURT: So she was a year older than you were?

THE DEFENDANT: Yes, sir.

THE COURT: Was she related to these people that you killed?

THE DEFENDANT: No, sir.

THE COURT: How was it that she became part of this criminal enterprise—endeavor?

THE DEFENDANT: Well, we had got high on some crack. Then—

THE COURT: Crack, meaning cocaine?

THE DEFENDANT: Yes, sir.

THE COURT: Where'd you get it?

THE DEFENDANT: A friend.

THE COURT: A friend?

THE DEFENDANT: He had got us high. And then we thought we would take the truck to go get some more drugs. So she was like, "Go get a knife." Then I had got the knife. Then I had remembered what she had told me. Then I had started stabbing my grandmoth—my grandmother. Then I had asked her to help me—

THE COURT: Wait a second. Wait a second. I want you to go back with me to the point that you said you were high, that your friend got you high. When was that? Was that on the day this happened?

THE DEFENDANT: The night before.

THE COURT: The night before it happened?

THE DEFENDANT: Early in the morning.

THE COURT: What time of the morning was it?

THE DEFENDANT: Probably around two o'clock.

THE COURT: Two o'clock in the morning? Where were you?

THE DEFENDANT: In Union City.

THE COURT: Union City?

THE DEFENDANT: Yes, sir.

THE COURT: Whereabouts in Union City, specifically?

THE DEFENDANT: I don't know.

THE COURT: You don't know?

THE DEFENDANT: (Shakes head.)

THE COURT: Were you at a house? Were you in a car? Were you outside?

THE DEFENDANT: In an apartment.

THE COURT: In an apartment.

THE DEFENDANT: (Nods head.)

THE COURT: Do you know whose apartment it was?

THE DEFENDANT: (Nods head.)

THE COURT: Whose apartment was it?

THE DEFENDANT: My friend Calvin.

THE COURT: Calvin?

THE DEFENDANT: (Nods head.)

THE COURT: And how old was he?

THE DEFENDANT: Thirty.

THE COURT: Thirty? How did you meet him?

THE DEFENDANT: A friend of the family.

THE COURT: A friend of whose family?

THE DEFENDANT: My mother's side.

THE COURT: A drug friend of the family—

THE DEFENDANT: (Nods head.)

THE COURT: —is that right?

THE DEFENDANT: Yes, sir.

THE COURT: Who introduced you to Calvin?

THE DEFENDANT: My mother.

THE COURT: Your mother?

THE DEFENDANT: (Nods head.)

THE COURT: How long had you known Calvin?

THE DEFENDANT: Just a few months.

THE COURT: A few months?

THE DEFENDANT: (Nods head.)

THE COURT: Did you get your drugs from Calvin?

THE DEFENDANT: Yes, sir.

THE COURT: This was crack cocaine?

THE DEFENDANT: Yes, sir.

THE COURT: Any other drugs?

THE DEFENDANT: Marijuana.

THE COURT: The same as your mother—

THE DEFENDANT: (Nods head.)

THE COURT: —is that right?

THE DEFENDANT: Yes, sir.

THE COURT: Any other type of drugs?

THE DEFENDANT: No, sir.

THE COURT: All right. So the night before this happened, you're with Calvin in his apartment in Union

City. It's about two o'clock in the morning. Calvin's thirty, you're fifteen and your friend's sixteen.

THE DEFENDANT: Yes, sir.

THE COURT: I presume she drove there.

THE DEFENDANT: He come and picked us up.

THE COURT: Where did he come to pick you up?

THE DEFENDANT: When you come out of my grandparents' driveway and you take a right, there's a little street right there called Travis Street in the neighborhood and we waited right there for him to come get us.

THE COURT: Who called him to come get you?

THE DEFENDANT: He called me and asked did I want to come over, and I said yes.

THE COURT: Now, you and the other young lady that participated, her name again is Sandy Ketchum?

THE DEFENDANT: Yes, sir.

(Pause in proceedings.)

THE COURT: What kind of relationship did you have with Sandy Ketchum, if any?

THE DEFENDANT: She was my—one of my best friends.

THE COURT: Where did y'all meet? In school?

THE DEFENDANT: Yes, sir.

THE COURT: Now, the night that you were over at Calvin's apartment, you said you got high on cocaine?

THE DEFENDANT: Yes, sir.

THE COURT: How long were you over his apartment?

THE DEFENDANT: All night, really, until—I knew that my grandparents got up at six o'clock so I didn't want them to think that I run away so I had told him—he said we were too messed up, that we needed to stay there. But I begged him to take me back around five-thirty.

THE COURT: Now, was it unusual that you stayed gone at night from your grandparents' home?

THE DEFENDANT: I had did it just a few times.

THE COURT: And what response did you get, if any, from your grandparents when you stayed out all night? I assume you didn't tell them where you were.

THE DEFENDANT: They didn't know.

THE COURT: They didn't know you were gone?

THE DEFENDANT: No, sir.

THE COURT: All right. This night that we're talking about, did they know you were gone?

THE DEFENDANT: No, sir.

THE COURT: So you were going to spend the night over at Calvin's doing drugs and then get back home before your grandparents got up in the morning at six o'clock—

THE DEFENDANT: Yes, sir.

THE COURT: —is that right?

THE DEFENDANT: (Nods head.)

THE COURT: Did you do that?

THE DEFENDANT: Yes, sir.

THE COURT: And did you get back to your grandparents' home?

THE DEFENDANT: Yes, sir.

THE COURT: And was Sandy with you?

THE DEFENDANT: Yes, sir.

THE COURT: Was anybody else with you?

THE DEFENDANT: No, sir.

THE COURT: How did you get back to the house?

THE DEFENDANT: Calvin drove us.

THE COURT: And he dropped you off?

THE DEFENDANT: Um-humm.

THE COURT: And did you go inside the house?

THE DEFENDANT: Yes, sir.

THE COURT: And where did you go when you went in the house?

THE DEFENDANT: To my room in the basement.

THE COURT: In the basement of your grandparents' home?

THE DEFENDANT: Yes, sir.

THE COURT: That's where you stayed?

THE DEFENDANT: Yes, sir.

THE COURT: And Sandy was with you?

THE DEFENDANT: Yes, sir.

THE COURT: Now, this is where I want you to explain to me fully how it was that you decided to stab your grandfather and grandmother.

THE DEFENDANT: Well, Sandy was like, "We should take their truck and we can get something to calm us down." I said— I didn't mean anything by it, but I was like, "We'd have to kill them to do that." But I didn't mean anything. Then she was like, "Well, we can hit them in the head with a lamp." And I was like, "Well, that might just make them pass out. Then they will wake up." She was like, "Go get a knife." So I had went and got a knife. And she was like— she had stabbed the bed to see if it was going to be sharp enough. She said it was sharp enough.

THE COURT: All right. Let me stop you right there. So you practiced stabbing?

THE DEFENDANT: (Nods head.)

THE COURT: Is that right?

THE DEFENDANT: Sandra did.

THE COURT: Did you stab anything other than the bed?

THE DEFENDANT: The wall.

THE COURT: Was anything on the wall?

THE DEFENDANT: A picture frame.

THE COURT: Was anything in the picture frame?

THE DEFENDANT: It was a painted picture of some puppies.

THE COURT: A painted picture of some puppies?

THE DEFENDANT: Yes, sir.

THE COURT: And you practiced and Sandy practiced stabbing the puppies?

THE DEFENDANT: She did.

THE COURT: Is that right?

THE DEFENDANT: Yes, sir.

THE COURT: Why?

THE DEFENDANT: To see— She was seeing if the knife was sharp.

THE COURT: Well, then why was it necessary to stab the bed also?

THE DEFENDANT: I don't know.

THE COURT: How many knives were there?

THE DEFENDANT: One at first. Then after it started, then I called her to help me.

THE COURT: All right. Wait a second. We're not there yet. I want to—

THE DEFENDANT: Okay.

THE COURT: —know everything about this. Do you understand me?

THE DEFENDANT: Yes, sir.

THE COURT: I haven't accepted your plea yet, and I want you to understand that.

THE DEFENDANT: Yes, sir.

THE COURT: All I've done is made a determination that your plea is free and voluntary.

THE DEFENDANT: Yes, sir.

THE COURT: Do you understand that?

THE DEFENDANT: (Nods head.)

THE COURT: And I've accepted the factual basis to accept the plea. But I want to satisfy myself that this is the correct thing to do; and what I'm hearing so far is— gives me a lot of concern about you. Now, you tell me about this knife. Who went and got the knife?

THE DEFENDANT: I did.

THE COURT: Where did you get the knife from?

THE DEFENDANT: From the kitchen.

THE COURT: And what type of knife was it?

THE DEFENDANT: The biggest one.

THE COURT: The biggest one?

THE DEFENDANT: (Nods head.)

THE COURT: You chose the biggest knife out of the kitchen?

THE DEFENDANT: (Nods head.)

THE COURT: Is that right?

THE DEFENDANT: Yes, sir.

THE COURT: And you took one knife, the biggest knife in the kitchen, back down to the basement, is that correct?

THE DEFENDANT: Yes, sir.

THE COURT: And you and Sandy practiced stabbing things to make sure the knife was sharp enough?

THE DEFENDANT: Yes, sir.

THE COURT: Sharp enough for what?

THE DEFENDANT: I guess to see, would it go—

THE COURT: Don't guess; you know. You were the one that did it.

THE DEFENDANT: To see if it would be sharp enough to stab them.

THE COURT: Stab them where?

THE DEFENDANT: Wherever the knife went. My eyes was closed the whole time.

THE COURT: All right. I assume at some point you satisfied yourself that the knife was sharp enough to do the job, is that correct?

THE DEFENDANT: Yes, sir.

THE COURT: Then what happened? There's still one knife, right?

THE DEFENDANT: (Nods head.)

THE COURT: You have the knife?

THE DEFENDANT: (Nods head.)

THE COURT: Is that right?

THE DEFENDANT: (Nods head.)

THE COURT: Your grandparents, for all you know, are sleeping, is that correct?

THE DEFENDANT: It's the middle of the day now.

THE COURT: It's the middle of the day now? All right. So you got home at what time?

THE DEFENDANT: Around five-thirty.

THE COURT: In the morning?

THE DEFENDANT: Yes, sir.

THE COURT: Well, you didn't practice for eight hours—nine or ten hours, stabbing pictures and beds, did you?

THE DEFENDANT: Because we didn't plan that at first.

THE COURT: Well, what did you do when you got home?

THE DEFENDANT: We just sat around in my room and listened to music.

THE COURT: What kind of music?

THE DEFENDANT: R and B, rap.

THE COURT: R and B and rap?

THE DEFENDANT: Yes, sir.

THE COURT: And you sat around for all day until you did this?

THE DEFENDANT: Yes, sir.

THE COURT: Never went out of your room?

THE DEFENDANT: To smoke cigarettes.

THE COURT: Anything else?

THE DEFENDANT: No, sir.

THE COURT: No more drugs?

THE DEFENDANT: (Shakes head.)

THE COURT: No marijuana?

THE DEFENDANT: We had a little bit left over. Then she— Sandy had told me to get them to come down there. So I had started smoking in the house so they would come downstairs.

THE COURT: Smoking what?

THE DEFENDANT: Some marijuana; the rest of the marijuana.

THE COURT: So they would come downstairs?

THE DEFENDANT: (Nods head.)

THE COURT: Why did you think they would come downstairs if you began to smoke marijuana in their house?

THE DEFENDANT: Because they could smell it.

THE COURT: Had you done that before?

THE DEFENDANT: No, sir.

THE COURT: But you thought they would be able to smell it—

THE DEFENDANT: Yes, sir.

THE COURT: —and then come downstairs?

THE DEFENDANT: (Nods head.)

THE COURT: And what was going to happen if they came downstairs?

THE DEFENDANT: Then Sandy had told me, when they come down there, start stabbing them.

THE COURT: All right. So let's get to mid-afternoon. You've got one knife, the big knife that you chose, that you figured out was sharp enough because of your practicing with it, to do what you were going to do?

THE DEFENDANT: (Nods head.)

THE COURT: And at this point you had already decided you were going to kill your grandparents, hadn't you?

THE DEFENDANT: Yes, sir.

THE COURT: Because a lamp might just knock them out?

THE DEFENDANT: Yes, sir.

THE COURT: So you wanted to kill them, is that right?

THE DEFENDANT: Yes, sir.

THE COURT: Why did you want to kill them?

THE DEFENDANT: (No verbal response.)

THE COURT: Had they ever done anything to you—

THE DEFENDANT: (Nods head.)

THE COURT: —other than raise you?

THE DEFENDANT: (Nods head.)

THE COURT: What?

THE DEFENDANT: Only the family knows. My grandmother used to scream at me and tell me all kind of things.

THE COURT: What kind of things?

THE DEFENDANT: She used to tell me that the only reason that I lived there was because— so I didn't go to DFACS [Department of Family & Children Services]. And when I was like ten, she used to call me a slut. And my grandfather, he hit me.

THE COURT: Was this why you decided to kill them?

THE DEFENDANT: No, sir.

THE COURT: Well, why'd you decide to kill them?

THE DEFENDANT: For Sandy.

THE COURT: I'm sorry?

THE DEFENDANT: For Sandy.

THE COURT: For Sandy?

THE DEFENDANT: (Nods head.)

THE COURT: You decided to kill your grandparents because of Sandy—

THE DEFENDANT: Yes, sir.

THE COURT: —or for Sandy?

THE DEFENDANT: (Nods head.)

THE COURT: Why?

THE DEFENDANT: I don't know.

THE COURT: You do know. Tell me.

THE DEFENDANT: So that we could be together.

THE COURT: What do you mean, you could be together?

THE DEFENDANT: We could leave.

THE COURT: Where would you go?

THE DEFENDANT: Anywhere.

THE COURT: Were you still in school during this period of time?

THE DEFENDANT: It was summer.

THE COURT: Well, you were out of school, but you were still a student, were you not?

THE DEFENDANT: Yes, sir.

THE COURT: And where were you going to school?

THE DEFENDANT: At Flat Rock.

THE COURT: What about Sandy?

THE DEFENDANT: I don't know.

THE COURT: Was she living with her parents?

THE DEFENDANT: Her mother.

THE COURT: Her mother?

THE DEFENDANT: (Nods head.)

THE COURT: And where did she live?

THE DEFENDANT: In Griffin.

THE COURT: In Griffin?

THE DEFENDANT: (Nods head.)

THE COURT: All right. So you began to smoke this marijuana cigarette to attract your grandparents downstairs so you could kill them for Sandy—

THE DEFENDANT: Yes, sir.

THE COURT: —is that right? Did you smoke?

THE DEFENDANT: Yes, sir.

THE COURT: Did your grandparents come downstairs?

THE DEFENDANT: They said they needed to get a suitcase because my grandmother was going to Hawaii. So I let them in—(pause)—and my grandfather was in the closet—(pause)—and I closed my eyes—(pause)—

THE COURT: Closed your eyes and did what?

THE DEFENDANT: I stabbed my grandmother.

THE COURT: While your grandfather was in the closet?

THE DEFENDANT: Yes, sir.

THE COURT: Where was your grandmother?

THE DEFENDANT: Standing beside the bed.

THE COURT: Was she facing you, or did she have her back to you, or were you side-by-side, or what?

THE DEFENDANT: I was looking at her and her—she was turning sideways and her back was sort of to me, but it was more a side.

THE COURT: Where was the knife while you were talking and letting them downstairs? Where did you have the knife?

THE DEFENDANT: Hid in the back of my pants.

THE COURT: What kind of pants did you have on?

THE DEFENDANT: Some jeans.

THE COURT: So you had it tucked in behind you?

THE DEFENDANT: Yes, sir.

THE COURT: Is that right?

THE DEFENDANT: Yes, sir.

THE COURT: Did you have a top on that went down over your jeans so that it would conceal the handle or the blade of the knife?

THE DEFENDANT: Yes, sir.

THE COURT: So you thought about hiding the knife, is that right?

THE DEFENDANT: No. No, sir. Just when they come downstairs, I had put it in behind my pants while they came in.

THE COURT: Where was Sandy?

THE DEFENDANT: Beside the bed.

THE COURT: All right. So your grandfather's in the closet looking for a suitcase?

THE DEFENDANT: (Nods head.)

THE COURT: Is that right?

THE DEFENDANT: Yes, sir.

THE COURT: Your grandmother's standing there in front of you. How far away from you is she?

THE DEFENDANT: About two feet.

THE COURT: You could reach out and touch her?

THE DEFENDANT: Yes, sir.

THE COURT: And then you said she turned so that her back was to you?

THE DEFENDANT: Yes, sir.

THE COURT: So tell me what happened when she turned and her back was to you.

THE DEFENDANT: That's when I remembered what Sandy said, so I closed my eyes and I stabbed her.

THE COURT: You closed your eyes and you stabbed her?

THE DEFENDANT: (Nods head.)

THE COURT: Do you know where you stabbed her?

THE DEFENDANT: In the back.

THE COURT: Do you know how many times you stabbed her?

THE DEFENDANT: Maybe three times.

THE COURT: All in the back?

THE DEFENDANT: (Shakes head.)

THE COURT: Well, when you stabbed her in the back, what happened the first time?

THE DEFENDANT: She made— She screamed, but it wasn't very loud. Then—

THE COURT: Show me, how long was this knife? Was it this long (indicating)?

Judge English raised his hands in front of him, suggesting the length of the knife as if he were indicating the length of a small fish he had just caught.

THE DEFENDANT: The blade was about this long (indicating).

Holly quietly spread the palms of her hands apart about ten to twelve inches and looked at English in embarrassment.

THE COURT: The blade was about this long (indicating).

Judge English, staring straight at her, mimicked Holly's gesture.

THE DEFENDANT: Yes, sir.

THE COURT: That's what, about eight to ten inches?

THE DEFENDANT: Yes, sir.

THE COURT: Now, when you stabbed her in the back, did you feel the blade go all the way in?

THE DEFENDANT: No, sir.

THE COURT: It did not go all the way in?

THE DEFENDANT: I don't know.

THE COURT: And then she screamed?

THE DEFENDANT: Yes, sir.

THE COURT: And then what happened?

THE DEFENDANT: My grandfather turned around and they were cussing and he had come and punched me in the face. And then he had me pinned down. So I was stabbing him, I guess in the— in the chest. And I had called Sandy to— to help me.

THE COURT: So did she help you?

THE DEFENDANT: (Nods head.)

THE COURT: And did she have a knife?

THE DEFENDANT: She— when they had seen her— because they didn't know she was there—they started cussing at her. And my grandfather ran upstairs. And she said, "Give me the knife." So I gave

her the knife. And she stayed downstairs with my
grandmother and I was standing there. And she said,
"Go get him." And first I was like, "No!" She said,
"Go get him, go get him, he's going to call 911." So I
had ran upstairs. And he had the phone in his hand.
Then I had pulled the cord out of the wall. Then he
had ran and grabbed a knife and I thought he was going to stab me. But I took the knife from— from my
grandpa and I closed my eyes and I just started stabbing my grandpa real fast. Then the last time that I
stabbed my grandpa, a lot of blood come on me.

THE COURT: A lot of blood came on you?

THE DEFENDANT: (Nods head.) Like— Like somebody just poured a big old bucket of hot water on
me. So I had let go. And I opened my eyes. And he
staggered and he— he walked around the kitchen
island and he fell on the kitchen floor.

THE COURT: Did you see where you had stabbed him?

THE DEFENDANT: When I looked down, it was in his
neck.

THE COURT: Where in his neck?

THE DEFENDANT: Right here (indicating).

THE COURT: On the right-hand side right there?

THE DEFENDANT: Yes, sir.

THE COURT: Is that where the blood came from when
you said it felt like a bucket of hot water?

THE DEFENDANT: I assume.

THE COURT: Do you know how many times you
stabbed him?

THE DEFENDANT: No, sir.

THE COURT: Did Sandy ever stab him?

THE DEFENDANT: No, sir.

THE COURT: Do you know how many times you stabbed your grandmother? You said three earlier, is that right?

THE DEFENDANT: Yes, sir.

THE COURT: Did Sandy stab your grandmother?

THE DEFENDANT: When we got in the truck, she told me that she was stabbing my grandma in the heart and in the back of the head and that she had cut some of the— some of the skin off of her arm.

THE COURT: So you left with Sandy—

THE DEFENDANT: (Nods head.)

THE COURT: —and you took the truck—

THE DEFENDANT: (Nods head.)

THE COURT: —that belonged to your grandparents, is that correct?

THE DEFENDANT: Yes, sir.

THE COURT: Where'd you get the keys from?

THE DEFENDANT: They were hanging on the hook.

THE COURT: Hanging on the what?

THE DEFENDANT: On the hook in the kitchen.

THE COURT: On the hook in the kitchen?

THE DEFENDANT: Yes, sir.

THE COURT: And then you and Sandy left, and where did you go?

THE DEFENDANT: We just started driving. First we tried to go back to Calvin's, but he was— I called his phone and he wasn't there.

THE COURT: Now, I assume at this time both of you had blood all over you.

THE DEFENDANT: She had— only had blood on her hands and her shoes, but I had it all over my face and all down the right side of my body.

THE COURT: So it's like you had just gutted a deer?

THE DEFENDANT: (Nods head.)

THE COURT: So, what, did you clean up at all or did you drive all the way to—Where was it, Mr. Ballard, Tybee Island?

MR. BALLARD: Yes, Your Honor.

THE COURT: —Tybee Island in that condition?

THE DEFENDANT: We didn't know where to go at first, but she said— she had got the phone and she called this girl named Sara Polk—and I had only met her once before—and we went to her house and she was on the phone and she got off the phone and we asked her, "Could we take a shower?" And she said no because her family had just pulled up, but she brought us a wet towel and told us to leave. Then she— she kept calling us and said it was on the news, trying to get us to tell her their names. But I hung up.

THE COURT: Did y'all still have the knives with you, or did you leave them at the house?

THE DEFENDANT: They were in the truck.

THE COURT: In the truck?

THE DEFENDANT: Yes, sir.

THE COURT: Why'd you take them with you?

THE DEFENDANT: Because they were the weapon. I thought we shouldn't leave them there.

THE COURT: So you ended up in Tybee Island?

THE DEFENDANT: (Nods head.) We didn't know where we was going. We just started driving.

THE COURT: All right. So you get to Tybee Island. Where did you stop in Tybee Island?

THE DEFENDANT: We seen this boy and his brother walking down the street. We asked them— We stopped and we asked them did they have another cigarette. So he gave us a cigarette and Sandy was like, "Where are you going?" And they said, "We just moved here today. We're going to the beach." And Sandy asked them could we walk with them. And they said yes. So we parked the truck in the lot and we started walking. We walked down the beach and we smoked some marijuana with them and they gave us a lot of pills. And we had told him— We didn't tell him what we did, but we told him that we ran away, but the truck was stolen. And he let us stay at his house for the night.

THE COURT: And you were eventually arrested by law enforcement from Fayette County, or do you know?

THE DEFENDANT: I don't know.

THE COURT: How long after you got down to Tybee was it that you were arrested?

THE DEFENDANT: Well, we spent the night, and the next morning his mother come down and she had asked could she use the cell— our cell phone to get theirs activated; and I didn't think anything, and I said yes. About ten minutes later [sic] she brought it back and I'd say it was about an hour he [one of the Clayton brothers] said, "The next-door neighbor's house is getting raided." And I had looked out the window and I didn't— I said, "I don't see any-body." Then me and Sandy looked at each other and I knew we was about to go to jail, so I had looked for somewhere to hide. Then the SWAT team had come in. And then they told us to get on the floor. So I got on the floor and they arrested me.

THE COURT: Anything else you're wanting to say?

THE DEFENDANT: No, sir.

MS. CHIDESTER: No, Your Honor.

THE COURT: You understand, if I accept this plea, what you're pleading guilty to?

THE DEFENDANT: Yes, sir.

THE COURT: And you understand the sentence that has been recommended to you, which is the only sentence a juvenile can get in the state of Georgia for something like this?

THE DEFENDANT: Yes, sir.

THE COURT: Do you understand that?

THE DEFENDANT: Yes, sir.

THE COURT: You're getting two life sentences, consecutive. That's the recommendation.

THE DEFENDANT: Yes, sir.

THE COURT: Do you understand what that is?

THE DEFENDANT: My lawyer tried to make it clear as she can, that I have to serve at least twenty years.

THE COURT: Twenty years?

THE DEFENDANT: (Nods head.)

THE COURT: That you have to serve at least twenty years.

THE DEFENDANT: Yes, sir.

THE COURT: At which time, do you realize that you will become eligible for parole?

THE DEFENDANT: No, sir.

THE COURT: Well, I don't know that anybody knows how the Pardon and Parole Board works. But, in any event, if it is twenty years, ten years for each life sentence—and I wasn't being derogatory about Pardon and Parole; I just don't understand how they work—

MS. CHIDESTER: No.

THE COURT: —how they compute sentences. But in the event you are eligible for parole in twenty years, that doesn't mean necessarily that you will be out in twenty years. You understand that?

THE DEFENDANT: Yes, sir.

THE COURT: But I guess there is a possibility that you could be out in twenty years and you do understand that?

THE DEFENDANT: Yes, sir.

THE COURT: So you think twenty years is a pretty good exchange for killing your grandparents?

THE DEFENDANT: (No verbal response.)

THE COURT: Is that a "Yes," or a "No," or "I don't give a damn"? What is it?

THE DEFENDANT: No, sir.

THE COURT: What do you think ought to be done to you?

THE DEFENDANT: I think I should be dead.

THE COURT: Well, we both agree on that, but the posture of the law is that a juvenile cannot be sentenced to death.

THE DEFENDANT: (Nods head.)

THE COURT: I've tried to think, in the thirty years I've been doing this, twelve of which was where Mr. Ballard is right now, eighteen of which has been as a judge, I've tried to think of another case that I have been involved with, connected with, or heard about that was, number one, as brutally savage as this was—and I've seen some hardened criminals come through court. And yet a fifteen-year-old little girl comes in front of me and admits to savagely killing the people she lives with. And I can tell you this, I can't— I can't think of another case in the thirty years that has been as nonsensical or as brutal as this. I think your description of the blood all over you like being drenched with warm water or a bucket of warm water is very descriptive of what went on that day. I can tell you this, and you won't remember this. You probably won't remember any of this once you get off into the prison system. If there was another alternative, a harsher alternative, for sentencing you, I'm sure Mr. Ballard would be requesting that. You are fortunate in that you were just a little too young for the full force of the law to be invoked. I say you're lucky. It may be worse that you spend the rest of your life or a lot of your life in prison; I don't know.

So have you and Sandy talked since that day?

THE DEFENDANT: No, sir.

THE COURT: Not at all?

THE DEFENDANT: No, sir.

THE COURT: So you don't know what's going to happen to her?

THE DEFENDANT: No, sir.

THE COURT: Don't care?

THE DEFENDANT: I care about her.

THE COURT: You care about your grandparents?

THE DEFENDANT: Yes, sir.

THE COURT: Have you talked to your mother?

THE DEFENDANT: Yes, sir.

THE COURT: Have you talked to Calvin?

THE DEFENDANT: No, sir. I don't want to.

THE COURT: Well, Miss Harvey, I will advise you, ma'am, that I will accept your plea, because that's the only thing we can give you.

THE DEFENDANT: Yes, sir.

THE COURT: On count number one of indictment number 04R-342—that is the indictment charging you with malice murder—I will sentence you to life imprisonment. On count number two of indictment number 04R-342—that charges you with malice murder—I will sentence you to a consecutive life sentence. So that you don't misunderstand this, you do understand that these life sentences are one after the other, consecutive?

THE DEFENDANT: Yes, sir.

THE COURT: Now, I've never understood this either, but I am obligated to advise you of a sentence review. I don't know that there's anything a sentence review panel could do on a life sentence, which is the minimum sentence and the maximum sentence. But for purposes of the record, I will advise you that you do have the right to have this sentence reviewed, and Ms. Chidester is familiar with the sentence review process. Now, let me ask Mr. Ballard, because I already know the answer to this, because he briefed me fully on what was getting ready to take place this morning, and one of his immediate observations and one of his immediate concerns were whatever family members are left, family members to the grandparents, and he advised me that they had been educated on what was going to take place, the sentence. And they, I think, were in agreement with the sentence. Is that correct, Mr. Ballard?

MR. BALLARD: That is correct, Your Honor. They are.

THE COURT: Ma'am, is there anything you want to say before you leave this courtroom?

THE DEFENDANT: I just hope that everybody can forgive me.

THE COURT: Ms. Chidester, anything, ma'am?

MS. CHIDESTER: No, Your Honor.

THE COURT: Well, I know it's been a very difficult case
for you to become involved with, but, Ms.
Chidester, let me thank you for the work you've
done. You've done—and people don't realize What
goes into these things to get to this point—but
you've done quite a bit of preparation. You've been
in my office a number of times requesting different
things, and you were prepared, I think, to go to this
trial on this should it—

MS. CHIDESTER: Yes, Your Honor.

THE COURT: —should it have to take place. And I
thank you for your efforts in this—

MS. CHIDESTER: You're welcome, Your Honor.

THE COURT: —in this regard. And, Mr. Ballard, I thank
you, too, for the expedient manner in which this
thing was put together. It was a complex, complex
case from the standpoint of just gathering the evidence, waiting for certain things to be returned to
you from an evidentiary standpoint.

MR. BALLARD: Well, thank you, Judge, but really, the
credit really goes to the Fayette County Sheriff's
Office. Within seventeen hours, despite the fact that
this, these girls were at the coast of Georgia, they
had them under arrest.

THE COURT: Well, lucky for me, my entire career has
been spent in the Fayette—or the Griffin Judicial
Circuit and I've been involved in traveling to Fayette
County for thirty years. My office has been in Fayette

County for eighteen years and I concur with what you say. Fayette County, from my perspective—and I've done a lot of traveling—has the most professional and best law enforcement in the state of Georgia, if not matching with anybody in this country of ours. And I'm not just talking about this case. But since you are giving credit to the Fayette County Sheriff's Department, the residents of Fayette County are indeed fortunate to have a sheriff like Randall Johnson and a staff like the Fayette County sheriff's department to protect them, because they are, again, some of the most professional people I have ever been around—professional people. And I've been involved in the military all my adult life, so I've been around a lot of military/law enforcement–type of individuals. And thank you for your comments, Mr. Ballard.

MR. BALLARD: Yes, sir, Judge. Several of them didn't go to sleep until they had them under— under— in custody.

THE COURT: Well, I'm glad they were the ones that were involved in the investigation, because, as you said, it was brought together in a very quick fashion, very professional fashion, and I think you're ready to go to trial if you had to right now.

MR. BALLARD: Oh, yes, sir.

THE COURT: Well, Miss Harvey, that's the sentence of the court, two life sentences. And you can take her out, please.

MR. BALLARD: Thank you, Your Honor.

THE COURT: Thank you very much.

The proceedings concluded, Holly Harvey was ig-
nominiously led manacled from the courtroom. The
gallery audience stood in silence. Once Holly disappeared behind a door with a pair of deputies, attention
and cameras appeared to be focused on her mother
Carla and Uncle Kevin in the first row of seats. There
was no sign of emotion as they stood together in their
sorrow. The sad saga was nearly concluded.

Scott Ballard wasn't sure if he could believe everything Holly had said. He was surprised by some of her
statements. Ballard hadn't known that someone had
supplied them with drugs the day of the murders. He
believed that Holly's account of the evening of August
2 cast a lot more blame on Sandy than was the case.

There wasn't really anything new in Holly's responses that Judy Chidester thought would influence
the plea bargain for Holly. Holly's revelation about the
fact they had smoked marijuana laced with cocaine the
day of the murders and the partial identity of the dealer
was explosive, but only in terms of the feasting media
and the sheriff's department. It had no real bearing on
the terms of the deal.

Chidester thought that Holly probably minimized
her culpability in the double homicide. She was sure
that Sandy would do the same in her hearing, which
was beginning momentarily. Self-preservation, after
all, was a basic instinct. Whether the tireless advocate
for the teenage murderer believed the full story about
what happened the night of August 2 at 226 Plantation
Drive would never be known. But did it matter? Two in-

nocent people were dead and two young girls would be spending a substantial part of their lives in jail atoning for it. It was a tragedy no matter how you looked at it.

Scott Ballard was left still wondering how the girls could commit such brutal, heinous murders, especially when the victims were Holly's elderly grandparents. Ballard took satisfaction in how quickly the case was solved by the sheriff's department and how quickly the girls were apprehended. He was rightly proud of them.

Ballard also thought the judges had done an excellent job, since they had had to set aside their usual schedules to handle these high-profile cases that had snowballed rapidly into the events of the last two weeks.

Judy Chidester found it interesting that, at the news conference that followed the hearing, Bruce Jordan remarked that certain things that Holly had said were "inconsistent with the evidence." There was nothing that proved, as Jordan suggested, that Holly was the ringleader and that love-struck Sandy was simply following her orders. Chidester thought it wouldn't have mattered anyway in the scheme of things, since both girls' conduct was "egregious," and there was more than enough guilt to go around.

Still Judy Chidester confessed that this plea was the most difficult one she had ever participated in, due to the fact that Judge English doggedly drew out every sordid detail of the murders. According to Chidester, English was "glaring at my client and obviously disgusted by her." When Judge English asked Holly what she thought should happen to her, she replied, "I should be dead." He had agreed with her. Chidester considers Judge English an old friend, but found his conduct "inappropriate."

Holly Harvey's lawyer felt her client had gotten the best deal she could possibly get. Holly saved herself at least an additional 10 years and as much as 18 years added on to the minimum of 20 years she got.

Holly and Chidester had discussed the reality of her sentence prior to the hearing. Understanding she would not be getting out of prison until at least her mid-30s, Chidester told her that she could still start a family, something that Holly had told her that she really wanted in life. She told Holly she should take advantage of every single program they offer in prison to better herself. That included not only educational programs, but ones that dealt with drug dependencies and psychological issues as well.

The proceeding and the events that led up to it had been exhausting for the soft-spoken grandmother. She went right home and collapsed on her bed. She remembers her son knocking on her door and asking if she had seen herself on the six o'clock news. She replied no and fell back to sleep.

Over the following weeks one sad thought haunted the defense attorney, who had thought she had seen it all. Carla Harvey, Holly's mom, now out of jail, had approached her after the hearing. Carla told Chidester that she had never been able to impart any meaningful life lessons to her daughter in the short and often interrupted time they spent together. But now she could: "I can teach her how to get along in prison."

◆ ◆ ◆

Dr. Greg Moffatt, a board-certified trauma specialist, an author of three books on homicide and violent behavior, professor of psychology at Atlanta Christian College, and a regular lecturer on homicide at the FBI Academy in Quantico, Virginia, sat in on Holly's and Sandy's allocutions. According to Moffatt, Holly showed little remorse and her words "rang hollow in light of her history of manipulation." He wrote, as a guest columnist in the Fayette County newspaper *The Citizen*, that she demonstrated in court that she has always been "a selfish and manipulative girl."

EIGHTEEN

Judge English grilled Holly Harvey for over thirty minutes in excruciating detail on what happened the night of August 2, 2004. The intense questioning was incredibly risky for both girls, because if Holly had said anything that English did not like, in an open courtroom with the media present, he was within his powers to throw out the plea bargain. Judge Johnnie Caldwell could have easily followed suit. Walker would then be faced with a trial on a case that would have already been thoroughly scrutinized by the media. He wondered how the girls would ever get a fair trial then.

After listening to Judge English question Holly as to whether she understood the charges against her and the plea bargains, Lloyd Walker breathed a sigh of relief and left Holly's hearing for the trial room next door. Holly had held up well under the withering questioning and "not screwed the deal." He believed that he and his client Sandy Ketchum were "almost out of the woods." Now Sandy's fate rested in the hands of Judge Johnnie Caldwell.

Lloyd Walker had a lot to fear facing Judge Johnnie Caldwell Jr. Like Judge English, Caldwell had a well-deserved record as an unsympathetic jurist when presiding over violent criminal and sex cases. Caldwell had won his most recent election by an impressive margin of 60 percent. His traditionalist law-and-order credentials served him well with the conservative electorate.

Judge Johnnie Caldwell Jr. hails from Upson County, Georgia. His father, Johnnie Caldwell Sr., was a very powerful politician in the "old" Democratic Party, when Dixiecrats ran things in the Deep South. Johnnie Sr. is reputed to be responsible for the rise of former governor, U.S. Senator and prominent national figure Zell Miller.

According to a long-time watcher of Georgia politics, the Caldwells were "movers and shakers in the old style" before the Republican Party wrestled power in the South from the Democrats.

Starting out as an attorney in Thomaston in Upson County in the late 1960s, he soon took a job as an ADA in the Griffin Judicial Circuit before getting elected district attorney. It is said his ambition was to be a judge.

In 1992 Caldwell was defeated by Fletcher Sams when he ran for re-election. Caldwell retreated to private practice for four years. He ran against Sams again in '96 and won back his seat. In 1997 Zell Miller appointed Caldwell to the bench when a civil rights lawsuit that had frozen all new judgeships was settled, and a fourth judge for the Griffin Judicial Circuit was authorized by the legislature.

Judge Johnnie Caldwell Jr. was from the "old

school," when a mean-spirited attitude pervaded the rural counties' judges and prosecutors. Caldwell was transparently pro-prosecution, no doubt due to his employment in that office. One source related that in his early years as a judge, Caldwell could be "mean as hell on the bench and abusive to both litigants and their lawyers." One lawyer reported that Caldwell told him: "If he thought he was tough, he [the lawyer] should have been around in the old days when he started." It was a time when many judges and prosecutors were tyrants and the violating of defendants' civil rights as we know them today was pervasive throughout the South.

Caldwell has mellowed in his years as judge, and the consensus of local lawyers is that he has grown from his old prosecutorial attitude and now shows a balanced approach to both prosecutors and defense attorneys. But as one local lawyer says, "People are still scared of him."

It is well-known in the local legal community that Judge Caldwell acquaints himself with the relevant law and is prepared when he takes the bench in a complex case, which is more than a lot of judges do. He reportedly has a good sense of humor and can be earthy in private, and has never been heard using racist language. As one lawyer related, "Deep down he's a good guy and a decent Christian."

In 2003 Judge Caldwell sat on the bench during the trial of Larry Wilson, which was watched with interest by the local media. Wilson was a certified nursing assistant at Sunbridge Nursing Home when he was accused of sodomizing a patient who was undergoing treatment at the home after suffering a stroke.

Wilson was fingered by two nurses at the long-term

treatment facility. One of them, Calandria King, testified that she'd witnessed the assault on the invalid while making her rounds. The other nurse, Christy Hinton, claimed the victim had told her, "He hurt me, he hurt me, he hurt me." Hinton went on to recount that the victim had identified the attacker as Larry Wilson. Wilson was quickly found guilty. Judge Caldwell showed no mercy even though Wilson had no criminal record for sex-related or violent crimes. He meted out the maximum sentence—23 years in a Georgia state prison.

Sandy Ketchum was escorted before Judge Caldwell by a female court officer from a side door in the front of the courtroom. She was dressed in a neon yellow prison smock and blue jeans, her hands cuffed in front of her. She had put on weight in her six months of languishing in jail waiting for this day. Her sad round face was framed by her brown hair, cut short and parted in the middle. Her hair appeared to be wet, as if she had just emerged from a shower. She took a seat at the defense table in the front, just to the right of the bench where Judge Johnnie Caldwell sat impatiently stroking his chin and glancing at his watch.

When the Harvey proceedings ended, Lloyd Walker had hurried over to join Sandy at the defense table. With the most apologetic tone he could summon, Walker informed the judge that DA Ballard was still in the English courtroom explaining Holly's plea. Caldwell impatiently asked, "Are we going to do a plea or not?" Walker stalled and nervously glanced at the door, anxiously awaiting the arrival of Scott Ballard.

As soon as Holly was officially sentenced, DA Ballard bolted the courtroom for the room next door. Caldwell, Walker, and Ballard went into the judge's chambers to discuss the plea. Both Walker and Ballard apologized for keeping the clearly aggravated Caldwell waiting. Ballard then explained the details of the plea bargain. That completed, the three men returned to the courtroom.

Scott Ballard stood just to the left of the bench facing the defense table and addressed Sandy Ketchum.

MR. BALLARD: Sandra Ketchum, would you come forth?

Sandy and Lloyd Walker rose and took their place behind a podium in front of the bench.

MR. BALLARD: Your correct name is Sandra Ketchum?

THE DEFENDANT: Yes, sir.

MR. BALLARD: Tell us your date of birth.

THE DEFENDANT: April nineteenth 1988.

MR. BALLARD: You are represented by Mister Lloyd Walker, is that correct?

THE DEFENDANT: Yes, sir.

MR. BALLARD: Are you satisfied with his services in this case?

THE DEFENDANT: Yes, sir.

MR. BALLARD: Is he advising you to your satisfaction regarding the facts of the case and the events available to you and the charges and the ranges of this case?

THE DEFENDANT: Yes, sir.

MR. BALLARD: Do you understand that you have been charged with one count of malice murder, one count of felony murder and one count of armed robbery? For a person your age, on those three offenses could be life sentences that you received, three consecutive life sentences for those offenses, do you understand that?

THE DEFENDANT: Yes, sir.

MR. BALLARD: Do you understand what you've been charged with, and the range of events against you?

THE DEFENDANT: Yes, sir.

MR. BALLARD: I have some other questions that I need you to speak out on, so that this court and court reporter can hear. Do you understand the nature of the events that you are charged with?

THE DEFENDANT: Yes, sir.

MR. BALLARD: Do you understand, by entering a plea of guilty, you waive the right to trial by jury and right to council at that trial?

THE DEFENDANT: Yes, sir.

MR. BALLARD: Do you also, by your plea, understand you waive the presumption of innocence?

THE DEFENDANT: Yes, sir.

MR. BALLARD: Do you understand, by that plea, that you waive the right to confront witnesses against yourself?

THE DEFENDANT: Yes, sir.

MR. BALLARD: Do you understand that you waive the right to subpoena witnesses at that trial?

THE DEFENDANT: Yes, sir.

MR. BALLARD: And you understand that you waive to testify and offer evidence at that trial?

THE DEFENDANT: Yes, sir.

MR. BALLARD: You understand you have the right not to incriminate yourself and by pleading not guilty or remaining silent and not entering a plea, you have a jury trial, but by entering a plea, you waive that right?

THE DEFENDANT: Yes, sir.

MR. BALLARD: Do you further understand the terms of the negotiating plea?

THE DEFENDANT: Yes, sir.

MR. BALLARD: Do you understand the recommendation made by the state may be accepted or rejected by the court?

THE DEFENDANT: Yes, sir.

MR. BALLARD: Do you understand the maximum possible sentence on the charge, including that possible and consecutive sentences and enhanced sentences provided by the law?

THE DEFENDANT: Yes, sir.

MR. BALLARD: Do you understand the mandatory minimum sentences depending on the charge?

THE DEFENDANT: Yes, sir.

MR. BALLARD: You are a citizen of the United States, is that correct?

THE DEFENDANT: Yes, sir.

MR. BALLARD: Are you under the influences of drugs or alcohol at the present time, so that you don't understand what is going on here today?

THE DEFENDANT: No, sir.

Judge Johnnie Caldwell took over the questioning of Sandy Ketchum.

THE COURT: Miss Ketchum, did anybody promise you anything to plead guilty to something you say that you are not guilty of?

THE DEFENDANT: Excuse me?

THE COURT: Did anybody promise you anything to get you to plead guilty to something that you say you are not guilty of here today?

THE DEFENDANT: No, sir.

THE COURT: Did anyone force or coerce you in any way to plead guilty to something that you say you are not guilty of here today?

THE DEFENDANT: No, sir.

THE COURT: All right, let me say, based on questions and answers that I've heard, based on the voluntariness of your plea, I do find that you are free[ly] and voluntarily entering a plea of guilty to these offenses without any threat or coercion or the benefit of reward, by the factual allegations concerning these pleas.

Scott Ballard took the floor once again.

MR. BALLARD: Now if we were to proceed to trial we would have shown on August second, 2004, that Sandra Ketchum and Holly Harvey basically lured Holly's grandparents, Carl Collier and Sarah Collier, into Holly's bedroom and, using knives, stabbed them to death and then stole the truck, took keys, and drove to, first, a friend's house and, later, Tybee Island, where within seventeen hours, they were apprehended by Fayette County sheriff's department and placed under arrest.

The judge resumed questioning of Sandy.

THE COURT: Is that true, ma'am?

THE DEFENDANT: Yes, sir.

THE COURT: Is that what you're pleading guilty to?

THE DEFENDANT: Yes, sir.

THE COURT: All right then, let me also say that, based upon the allegations stated in the record, as well as your admission to guilt to those offenses, I do find that you're guilty of these. Is there anything anyone would like to say before I set the sentence in this?

MR. BALLARD: Yes, on behalf of the state I want to explain our recommendations to her. Our recommendations, of course, are one life sentence concurrent on each of those three charges. The reason we are only recommending one life sentence is—there is [sic] several reasons—one is that Miss Ketchum immediately cooperated with the police. Secondly she entered this plea, and had agreed that she would give testimony against Holly Harvey, had there been a trial for her. And third she, from the beginning, unlike Holly Harvey, showed significant remorse for her actions. Based on those factors—And it's my belief that her willingness to enter this plea and to testify against Holly induced Holly to accept the offer of consecutive life sentences. Based on that, we recommend the sentence be accepted.

THE COURT: But the law enforcement and victims' family?

MR. BALLARD: Yes, Your Honor, we have consulted with the victims' family, and they are in accord with this recommendation and similarly we have consulted with law enforcement and they are in accord with it as well.

MR. WALKER: Your Honor?

THE COURT: Yes, sir?

Lloyd Walker deferred to his client, who stood next to him at the podium.

THE DEFENDANT: I'd just like to say that if everything were right and I could take their place and pay back them my life, I wouldn't think twice, and I'm real sorry that this happened.

THE COURT: Let me say, ma'am, that I've done this for a long period of time, in some capacity for some thirty-three years, ma'am, and it behooves me that I don't understand the violence that people commit one to another, particularly violence that young people such as yourself and the other young woman did on, certainly, two innocent individuals, but also two elderly individuals, who certainly were not, probably, able to defend themselves, had they wanted to in this instance.

Having been the district attorney here for fifteen years and on the bench ten, and having tried twenty-two death penalty cases in my tenure, I would have no problem, had the law allowed us to do so, to have tried you for the death penalty in this case. However, that cannot be done because of your age, likewise because of state laws as well as the recommendations. Let me also say to you that if it were not for the recommendation of the district attorney, law enforcement, as well as the victims in this case, I would not accept this. I would give you five consecutive life sentences, I would tell you right now.

On this count two of malice murder, I will sentence you to life in prison. On count three, which is the other felony murder, I will sentence you to life in prison and that will run concurrent.

On this armed robbery, which carries ten to twenty or up to life, I am going to sentence you to serve life to that as well and that will also run concurrent with these other offenses.

Now you have the right to have this sentence reviewed by a sentence review panel. That is a panel of superior court judges who meet periodically in Atlanta to see if I've been too harsh on you. Of course, life is all you can get on the murder offenses; you could get from ten to twenty on the armed robbery. They can reduce that sentence if they wanted to. If you want to avail yourself to that, I will ask your attorney to help you with that. You also have certain rights concerning your right of habeas corpus. You can discuss that with your attorney, things of that nature, and any other type you feel that you may have.

You can take her out.

Sandy Ketchum, escorted by court officers, left the courtroom without a word.

From the moment the accused was led into the courtroom to the time she exited as a sentenced murderer, only twelve and a half minutes had elapsed.

Judge Caldwell handled the plea hearing along the usual lines where the defendant wasn't asked a lot of questions on the details of the murders. English deviated from the norm and Caldwell followed it. Ballard thought that both ways were "appropriate." Sandy, after all, had given the police a full statement upon her arrest.

In their court appearances, Dr. Greg Moffatt saw a totally different type of personality in Sandy Ketchum than in Holly Harvey. He believed Sandy to be "truly remorseful," and believed her to be the "follower—and followers often do things they would not do under different leadership." He went on to explain it this way:

"If Ketchum had chosen to follow a star student, or if she had hooked up with an Eagle Scout, her life would have taken a very different turn. This truth will become evident to her over time, and the decisions that led to her relationship with Harvey will haunt her for the rest of her life."

But Moffatt went on to write that whether Sandy was truly remorseful was a "tangential issue." Both girls had to realize that they had to be held accountable for what they'd done.

Moffatt realized that each judge had to make his own decision about whether the defendant before him was believable. They knew that from the time the girls had been incarcerated, they would have picked up knowledge on how the legal system worked. The girls also would have had council and coaching from their lawyers. In other words, they would have been prepared for their reckoning. Still, it appears that Dr. Moffatt lays the lion's share of blame for the murders squarely on Holly Harvey's shoulders.

Kevin Collier was standing beside his sister in the hallway outside the courtrooms when Sheriff Randall Johnson walked over. He expressed his condolences to Kevin for the loss of his parents. Kevin thanked him. Johnson never looked at or spoke to Carla. He quietly walked away. Miffed, Carla called after him, "They were my parents too!" Johnson never looked back.

It had been hard for Kevin to listen to the allocutions of his niece and Sandy Ketchum. The facts of the murders were horrific enough, but knowing they were committed by someone his parents and he had all loved made it particularly painful. Kevin was grateful the process had not taken the estimated two weeks that a drawn-out trial would have lasted. It spared him the dreaded experience of seeing the crime-scene photos and hearing the forensic evidence. Emotionally, that experience would have been devastating.

Kevin had not spoken to Holly since the murders, but he knew he eventually would. After all, "she was still family." He had been asked by friends if he would take her in were Holly to be let go the next day. It was a difficult question to answer for him, but he thought he probably would, saying, "I don't think she was in her right mind. I do believe they were on drugs."

Pausing for a moment, he added, "And, I still love her."

The lawyers, Bruce Jordan, Kevin Collier, and his sister Carla Harvey, assembled a few blocks away in the sheriff's office for a press conference after both hearings had ended. Immediately a question was fired at Carla about whether she felt responsible for what her daughter Holly had done. Her response was that she didn't feel "sorry for anything," adding that she took no responsibility for what had happened and that "it was all Holly's doing." Holly, Carla said, "was old enough to make her own decisions."

If the press was hoping for a mea culpa from the frequently jailed mother of the recently confessed murderer, they were disappointed.

The reporters pressed her for the full name of the mysterious drug dealer, Calvin. Carla refused to give it up. Bruce Jordan then leaned over and whispered into Kevin's ear, "She's not leaving this building until she gives us that last name."

Kevin remembered that when Holly had told Judge English about Calvin, Carla, sitting next to him in the courtroom, had uttered, "Uh-oh." She then muttered several times, "I'm dead, I'm dead." It was an overstatement of her predicament, but the often-arrested 37-year-old knew she would be facing more jail time if she was not forthcoming with the drug dealer's name and whereabouts. Carla Harvey, under questioning by Detective Ethon Harper, gave up the name.

Within twenty-four hours of learning the identity of the dealer who'd sold drugs to Holly and Sandy the day of the murders, sheriff's deputies arrested Calvin Lawson, 41, of Union City over in the adjacent Clayton County. Prior to Holly's sworn testimony in court, the police had been unaware of the involvement of

Lawson in the events surrounding the murders. He was charged with one count of felony murder in the deaths of Carl and Sarah Collier. Carla told police she had met Lawson when she had worked as a stripper at the Union City club The Gold Coast. Carla speculated that her daughter Holly must have met Lawson when he had stopped by her place. She claimed she had no knowledge of how Holly had learned he was a dealer.

On Wednesday, April 20, in what the local Fayette County newspaper *The Citizen* called a surprise move, the Fayette County Sheriff's Office officially dropped the felony murder charge against Calvin Lawson. But Calvin Lawson's legal troubles were far from over in regard to the Collier murders. County officials instead charged him with two counts of misdemeanor contributing to the delinquency of minors and one count of furnishing harmful materials to minors. He was also charged with furnishing harmful materials for allegedly showing the two minors pornographic material and soliciting sexual favors. Lawson posted a $1,950 cash bond and was released from police custody. Lieutenant Belinda McCastle of the sheriff's department was quoted in *The Citizen*:

> We dropped the murder charge because the weight of the testimony was going to be on Holly Harvey and Sandy Ketchum. There really wasn't enough to make our case stick, but we are going to continue our investigation and revisit that charge when the grand jury is in session in July [2005].

Lieutenant McCastle also said that the sheriff's department had "some evidence," but felt it was not sufficient at the time to hold Lawson on the more serious charges.

NINETEEN

For Holly Harvey and Sandy Ketchum the next twenty or more years behind bars will not be easy ones. The two girls can expect to be moved around a lot in the Georgia penal system. They will become very familiar with several detention centers within the state. Each one will have a different set of rules and a hierarchy amongst the inmates. It will be a difficult time of adjustment for the teenagers. Once they find a permanent home in the system at 21 years of age, they will find still another period of adjustment as they prepare to serve their lengthy sentences.

According to criminal justice expert Dr. Greg Moffatt, as perpetrators of particularly heinous crimes, they can expect to be bullied by other prisoners in the *de facto* justice system that they will find in place behind the walls and bars that will house them. Amidst this atmosphere, they will have to learn and adjust to survive. Moffatt writes:

They can expect that the system, even though it is called "correctional," is more about management and punishment rather than correction. There are no friends in prison and there is no trust in prison.

Other than mail correspondence, the two girls will never see each other again while in prison. They will never be in the same prison at the same time.

According to Dr. Moffatt the little things we all experience in everyday life will not be something that they can expect to know. Visiting loved ones will be separated from the teens by bullet-proof glass while talking to them over a telephone. Feeling the caress or a caring touch of a parent will be forbidden. Moffatt elaborated:

> These girls won't be able to stay up late if they want to sleep in. They won't be able to get a glass of milk from the refrigerator, watch a television show on their own TV, or enjoy a quiet book on a grassy hillside.

The sunshine on their faces and even a private visit to the toilet will become just memories.

According to Dr. Moffatt the hardest thing of all for the two girls will be having to face up to the enormity of what they've done. Even with the reality of their convictions it's unlikely they understand how the murders of the elderly couple will affect their lives so early on in their life in jail:

> They will miss much of what many of us remember most fondly from our youth: the prom, dating, our first

job, and high school graduation. They traded this away in a few impulsive minutes. As they mature, they will become ever more aware of the broad ramifications of taking a life. Grief and remorse could easily overwhelm them. This will become more evident as they watch their own child-bearing years slipping away and they will realize they might never have families of their own. They took life, but they may never be able to give life. This truth won't fully be realized for years.

Dr. Moffatt doubts the two will be granted parole the first time they are eligible. Historically Georgia's Pardon and Parole Board is reluctant to grant early releases. Even if they are released at the first opportunity, they will emerge from behind bars with nothing. They will have no money, no job skills, no social contacts to help them succeed, and only minimal education.

There is some hope for the girls: rehabilitation. But, says Moffatt, they must want it. "In twenty years Harvey and Ketchum will have to become what they decide to become. It won't be the system's fault, the judges' fault, or some attorney's fault."

Moffatt takes issue with one of the more dramatic exchanges between Holly and Judge English when he'd asked her if twenty years was "a pretty good exchange for killing your grandparents." Holly had answered that she "should be dead." English responded by saying, "Well, we both agree on that."

"The lust for revenge," Moffatt says, makes it easy to wish ill to the teenagers. Yes, justice must prevail, but one should hold out hope that people can change. After examining the girls' sad and tormented childhoods, an their lives on the days that led up to the horrible events of August 2, 2004, that change will not come easy.

District Attorney Scott Ballard was asked about the prospect of Holly and Sandy eventually walking the streets of Fayetteville again, some twenty years from now.

"I'm frightened on several levels," the DA said. "I'm personally frightened at the thought of either of these girls being at large unless they change significantly."

To Dr. Moffatt it is a reasonable fear, but he believes "significant change" is possible, citing several "amazing transformations" he has witnessed in cases just like this one.

There will be opportunities for the girls to improve themselves in prison, where they can develop educationally, spiritually, and socially, but they will have to want them and actively pursue them. Even though a large portion of their childhood and early adulthood will have been lost, at 30 years of age, the majority of their lives will still be ahead of them. If the two girls accept the "unconscionable act" they committed "regardless of the culpability of the other," there will be hope for them.

Not only were the mainstream media consumed with this story of misguided youths who were involved in a homosexual relationship and killed loved ones, but so was the alternative press that catered to the left and right of the political spectrum.

The gay press, including the high-profile *Advocate* ⌐d online news sources such as Gay.com and the re-⌐ *Southern Voice*, dutifully reported the story and ⌐d that Holly Harvey and Sandy Ketchum were lesbian lovers. Little else was written on the subject. The conservative press was, however, all over the story.

In his column in the web-based Accuracy in Media, Cliff Kincaid wrote that the mainstream media were "disguising the true facts" of the case out of "Fear of offending the homosexual lobby." He accused his colleagues in the big city papers such as *The Atlanta Journal-Constitution*, the Associated Press (AP) and the TV networks of painting the girls as merely "involved in a romantic relationship." Kincaid wrote that many in the media avoided the word "lesbian." He went on to write that the ponderous question being posed by the media on "Why Teens Kill" may have more insidious answers. Kincaid opined:

"Perhaps some of the answers lie in Hollywood and the media. Lesbianism is being depicted as part of growing up, and when the lifestyle leads to brutal murder, in conjunction with drug abuse, society is being blamed. The lives of real people are being destroyed . . ."

Tybee Island residents Patricia Pelleiren and her two sons were irate about how the Fayette County Sheriff's Office tried to "put a spin" on their involvement in the case at the time of the arrests. Pellieren thought the police were trying to imply that they had somehow known the girls even though their previous home in Barrow County was a good two hours away from Fayette County. The police also made veiled threats against them, since the two boys had admitted smoking marijuana with the girls.

The family was bombarded and pestered by the media for their story and Patricia had to be put on a leave of absence from her job at the hospital, losing two weeks of pay from a job she had just started. It was all, she says, because of "those crazy dang girls who killed the grandparents."

Patricia Pellieren also believed it was because of her forty-five-minute use of Holly's stolen cell phone, activating hers, that the police were able to pinpoint Holly and Sandy's whereabouts. Patricia also believed that if Brian had not run out of the house to get the cops' attention, the capture of the girls would have been delayed and not have gone as smoothly as it did. She feels she is owed a debt of gratitude rather than the abuse she and her kids had gotten.

Pellieren didn't think they were ever in much danger while the girls were in her house. At the time she had over $5,000 in cash and "lots" of jewelry lying about, and big diamond rings on her fingers. The real cost they paid, according to the single mother, was her elder son's mental well-being.

With the constant badgering by the police and the media, Brian became a "nervous wreck" with the accusations that he'd known what Holly Harvey and Sandy Ketchum had done. Brian believed the trouble the incident caused was his fault, because, after all, it was he who let the girls in. He also believed the police when they said his family would have been their next victims. The guilt was overwhelming. His nurse mother could see he had developed a "social anxiety" problem. Brian finally told his mother he couldn't take it anymore and wanted to kill himself. That was all she needed to hear. Pellieren immediately had her son admitted to the hospital.

The pressure did not let up. People drove up to their house and would stop and wander around. When they were at restaurants people were constantly watching and pointing and talking out loud about them. As the trial dates approached, they were called numerous times by the police, checking up on their whereabouts and informing them they should prepare to give testimony in the Fayette County courts. "Thank God the girls took the plea bargain deal and we didn't have to travel down to Thomasville, Georgia, to testify, which would have ruined our lives even more," Pellieren related.

After the sentencing, things have been "relatively quiet" for the Tybee Island family who got caught up in the wave of trouble. Pellieren has made it clear to her sons that they were not to talk to people from off the island. Strangers were not to be trusted. If they meet pretty girls on the beach, she tells her sons, find out first if they are vacationers. If they are, the boys should immediately "just walk away."

Patricia Pellieren had always tried to emulate her mother, whom she called a caring, generous woman, a "saint." Patricia donated time to charitable organizations and money to the less fortunate regularly. Because she's "her mother's daughter" and a registered nurse, Patricia loves helping people, and she believes her sons are that way too. That is why they helped the two fugitive girls who had no place to go, no money, and no food to eat. Now they are more reluctant to help people, because, says Pellieren, "people don't go around with a sign on them that says they are bad people." The whole episode was a frightening wake-up call for the self-described "people's person."

Trouble with the law continues to haunt Sandy's maternal side of the family. Everett McConnell, Sandy

Ketchum's half-brother by her mother's first marriage, tried to poison Sandra and her then current boyfriend Kenny Maddox in 1999. Everett was sent to prison for attempted murder. Sandra (Ketchum) Maddox was convicted of cruelty to children second degree on February 4, 2004 and sentenced to 5 years in prison. After being released on probation she was arrested for possession of methamphetamine and marijuana on July 19, 2005, and later sentenced to an additional two years. She is currently serving time in the Spalding County Jail. Ironically Sandra may eventually be transferred to the same prison her daughter Sandy is in to serve out her sentence.

Holly's father, Gene Harvey, continued to have problems with the law as well. Besides the theft of Kevin Collier's identity he was charged multiple times with crimes ranging from DUIs, to burglary, and escape from jail. He reportedly lives with his dad in Spalding County.

Everything that Tim and Beth Ketchum had accumulated from the day they got married to the present is now lost because of what happened the night of August 2, 2004. Married for four years, the struggling couple had moved into a four-bedroom house and, just two weeks prior to that fateful night, had finally acquired a second car. Beth Ketchum had woken up every morning at 5:30 A.M. and gotten Tim to work, returned home and gotten Sandy off to school, gone home again and showered and dressed and gotten herself to work. Everything, it seemed, that they had to buy was for Sandy. According to Beth, she got fired from three jobs because of all "the running around" she'd had to do for

Sandy, which entailed getting her counseling, and the probation hearings that were needed for her prior troubles with school and the law.

The Ketchums were now living with a cousin of Tim's. They had almost completed an agreement for the rental of a house when the landlord saw them on TV and reneged on the deal.

Tim and Beth Ketchum see Sandy every weekend. All things considered, they say, Sandy is adjusting to a life behind bars reasonably well. She had to be put on medication so she could sleep at night after bouts of nightmares that had her screaming herself awake. Sandy has told her parents she also suffers from flashback visions which terrify her, and that she can't seem to rid herself of the smell of blood that flowed profusely at 226 Plantation Drive the night of August 2, 2004.

Sandy is, however, hopeful for her future. While incarcerated and waiting for the fateful hearing of April 14, she had come to the conclusion that she wouldn't emerge from behind bars for forty to fifty years. That was reinforced by stepmother Beth, who claims she never withheld anything from Sandy. She'd told the 16-year-old that if her case went to trial, "the jury would burn her ass." But Sandy knew that "burning her ass" wouldn't come in the form of a death penalty, because of her age. It would just mean a lot of years in jail.

Sandy Ketchum has signed up for her GED classes with the intent of getting her high school degree. She has dreams of becoming a counselor for kids who have been in her situation. She has expressed over and over again to her parents that she wishes she had been killed instead of the Colliers, and that if she could, she would gladly give her life in exchange for theirs.

Tim and Beth can only take one small bit of consolation out of this whole tragic situation. Now they know where their little girl is, and that she'll be reasonably safe behind the walls that will be her only home for the next twenty years.

Sandy Ketchum has found a voice for her thoughts and feelings in verse. The teenager had always taken to the pen in the past. Her lonely life behind bars has provided plenty of time for reflection and it is clear she still thinks of Holly and of what she did.

"THINKING FIRST"

Sitting back,
Hearing the conversations
Wanting to relax
But am powered by temptation.
Wanting to react, in all kinds of ways.
But turning my cheeks
To sit in a daze.

Taking a few breathes,
Let it slip away
Praying to God
Asking for a better day.
Putting on a smile,
Saying I'm just fine
But knowing deep down
I'm having a hard time.

Remembering what I've done,
Wishing it weren't true
Shedding all these tears
Cause I did it all for "You."
Giving up my freedom
To love just one. . . .
It wasn't even worth it,
But it's already done.

Wanting to give my life,
So they could live again.
But knowing they're gone,
And I'm stuck in the pen.

Sandy Ketchum

Judy Chidester calls Holly from time to time to see how she is doing. Holly is always eager to talk. She had worriedly asked her legal counsel before the hearing if she would continue to hear from her after it was all over. Or would she "stop having anything to do with me?" It made the twenty-year veteran of the legal trenches sad that Holly had to ask. Holly begged her not to abandon her, and Chidester assured her she wouldn't. She promised to maintain contact, although not as much as they had had leading up to the disposition of the case.

Holly Harvey says she sees a lot of juveniles come and go into her facility. Most are in for minor offenses such as drug charges. Holly mentioned that from what these transient young female offenders tell her, she thinks the media and the public have made out that what she had done was worse than it actually was.

Chidester tried to explain that it was that bad, and no one could possibly make it out to be worse than it was.

Holly always asks her lawyer if she might be eligible for parole before 20 years. Chidester always tells her she doubts it, adding it's also hard to predict what the Pardon and Paroles Board will do ten years from now. A lot will depend, Chidester tells her, on how well she does in prison, how she copes, and if she gets into any kind of trouble. There will be plenty of rules to obey, many of them silly, but she will have to abide by them nevertheless if she has any real hope of an early release.

ages of 13 and 16. Of the jail population, 140 of the adult inmates between the ages of 17 and 20 were deemed too vulnerable to be housed with the general population. The segregation of prisoners did not save Wayne Boatwright Jr., 18, who was strangled to death in February 2004. The prison was reported to be the second most dangerous facility in the state.

Besides the murder of Boatwright (a wrongful death suit was settled with the Boatwright family) the Georgia Department of Corrections (DOC), according to *The Atlanta Journal-Constitution*, came under intense pressure to curb incidents of rape and violence at Alto. The Southern Center for Human Rights in Atlanta, after documenting dozens of incidences of fights, beatings, sexual assaults, and "other violence," asked the federal court to force DOC to do something.

Commissioner James Donald of the DOC "upon review and recommendations of my staff" and "economics," announced that DOC would be changing the "mission"—the prison. As of April 1, 2005, Alto became a women's prison. Sandy Ketchum became its first high-profile inmate in June 2005.

November 2005. Metro State Women's Prison, Atlanta, Georgia

Sandy was used to being uprooted. In her last three years on the outside she had moved seven times. Since starting kindergarten, she had attended ten different schools. At 16 years of age Sandy had a rap sheet that listed nine crimes. In October, Sandy was again uprooted. Without explanation, or informing her lawyer, she was moved to the Metro State Women's Prison in southeast Atlanta.

The Georgia Department of Corrections continued to refuse all my requests to interview Sandy, still insisting that she would have to be in jail for a year before they would consider any requests from the media. This was despite the fact that she was now considered an adult and had put me on her visitors' list.

Left only one other option, Sandy agreed to answer my questions in letter form about her life, her relationship with Holly Harvey, the crimes, and her life behind bars. Her lawyer, Lloyd Walker, presented her with the questions on one of his visits with her. She wrote, in her neat mixed-script and block lettering, the following candid and revealing response. The questions and bracketed questions and phrases are mine.

QUESTIONS FOR SANDY

[1] What are your earliest memories as a child?

[2] Do you recall your first stepmom? What about her?

[3] Do you remember your second stepmom? What about her?

[4] How was your relationship with your dad? What did you love about him? What did you hate?

[5] You moved around a lot. What was that like?

[6] All the different schools. Did you ever adjust to any of them?

[7] How would you describe your relationship with stepmom Beth?

[8] Was she tough?

[9] Do you think she loves you?

[10] How did you meet Holly? How did that go?

[11] How long did it take for you two to develop a romantic relationship?

[12] How long had you known you were gay?

[13] Were you loyal to her or did you screw around?

[14] Did Holly plan her grandparents' murders? How long in advance?

[15] Did she tell you? Did she ask for help?

[16] Tell me what you remembered on the day of the murders.

[17] Why did you drive to Sara Polk's?

[18] What was the drive down to Tybee like?

[19] What happened when you met up with the Clayton brothers on Tybee?

[20] What do you remember about the bust on Tybee?

[21] Tell me about your interrogation by Det. Jordan.

[22] What was jail like that first night?

[23] What about your arraignment?

[24] Did you get a chance to see your parents?

[25] How was the adjustment to jail? Can you give me some instances that stick out?

[26] Did you have any communications with Holly? What was said?

[27] Has Lloyd Walker been good for you?

[28] I saw the video of your sentencing. What are your memories of it?

[29] Do you think the judge was fair?

[30] Do you think the sentence was fair?

[31] Were you genuinely sorry for what you did?

[32] Do you blame all this on Holly?

[33] What was Alto like? Can you tell me some stories about the place?

[34] Why were you transferred back to Metro?

[35] Have you heard from Holly?

[36] Do you still feel for her?

[37] How do you plan to spend your time in Jail? School?

[38] When you get out what do you plan to do?

[1] *My earliest memories as a child at 4 or 5 was when I got my first electric jeep and first bike* [2] *Yes, I recall my first step mom. I thought she was my real mother. She got 2 tumors in her head and had brain surgery. The first surgery made her mean and the second surgery made her into a vegetable. She was the best thing that ever happened to me until her and my dad divorced. They made an agreement to split up if that ever happened. I still went to see her through the years before I got locked up. She has a son too.*

[3] *Yes! I remember my 2nd step mom too. She was the devil. My dad was with her for 3 or 4 years. She hated me for no reason at all. She beat me for the whole time they were together. I even called defax [DFACS—Department of Family & Children Services] on her and they took pictures of my bruises and still believed her over me. She messed my life up. I could never do anything right in her eyes. She has a daughter of her own and a daughter by my dad. When my dad woke up and finally realized what was going on we left her. I haven't seen my baby sister since she was two years old and she'll be six years old December 29th.*

[4] *My relationship with my dad was good. We were like best friends all my life. I loved that I could talk to him*

about anything. He was my shoulder when I needed to cry and basically my backbone. I hated that he didn't believe me when I told him about my 2nd step mom beating me. And also the fact that he would party a lot and leave me with my grandmother.

[5] *Moving around a lot was devastating to me.* [6] *Yes! I got comfortable in the schools I was at but usually when I got comfortable is the time we would move again.* [7] *My relationship with Step-mom Beth is beyond great. She is all the mom I've ever needed. She is also my best friend. I can talk to her about any and everything. I love her with all my heart and more.* [8] *Yes! She was tough at times but it was only for my own good. She really tried to help me change my life but me being stubborn didn't help the situation much.* [9] *I don't think she loves me, I know she does.*

[10] *I met Holly at school in the 8th grade in 2002. We were friends for a while and eventually turned into lovers.* [11] *I think it took 6 months to a year for us to develop a deep romantic relationship.*

[12] *I have known I was gay ever since I was a child. I knew something was different about me because I always hung around more boys than girls. I also didn't look at boys the way other females do. I found myself looking at females the way females look at males.* [13] *I was more than loyal to Holly. I never even thought twice about looking at another female when we were together but for her it was the other way around.*

[14] *My lawyer [Lloyd Walker] told me that the grandparents' son said that Holly had threatened to kill them the week before it happened.* [15] *Before it*

happened I would've never thought she was even thinking about something so hideous. She just didn't seem like that kind of person so, to my knowledge at the time it wasn't pre-planned.

[16] *Before it had came to the surface I was packing my stuff and about to leave because I was tired of going over there every weekend without them [Carl and Sarah Collier] knowing and tired of risking myself to go back to jail. When I went to walk out the door she said no don't leave so me being in love I didn't leave. I had to get out of there so I said lets steal the truck tonight and leave but then she turned around and said "I just wanna kill em." I laughed it off because I didn't think she was for real. When it went down I guess that's when I believed her. I was beside the bed scared to death. She kept calling my name and calling my name and I just kept laying there. Then she cried out for help one more time. So I jumped up and seen what was happening and tried to stop them by yelling, crying, and screaming "ya'll need to stop, please stop," but they looked at me like I didn't exist.*

Then I tried to get the knife from Holly so I struggled with that, then I stabbed her grandmother twice, once in the arm and once in the head, I really felt like I had no choice to do what I did. It was like I blanked out cuz after I stabbed her it was like I couldn't do anything, see, move, talk and even breathe. When I snapped out of it I noticed that Holly and her grandmother were gone and the only place they could've went was up the stairs so I ran up the stairs and about the time I turned to go

where they were that's when I saw them. Her grand-
father throws a green glass cup at me so I turned
my head so it wouldn't hit me in the face and about
the time I turned back around that's when Holly
stabbed her grandfather in the neck. Then he stum-
bled to the island in the kitchen, put his hand on the
counter, looked at me and said "OH SHIT" and fell
right in front of me. Then I blanked out again.

When I came out of it Holly was running back to
the kitchen and I said "let's get the hell out of
here" so we ran down stairs and on the way down
her grandmother was laying at the bottom of the
stairs and I told Holly "you're grandmother is still
breathing leave her alone and lets get the hell outta
here." She went down there and tried to stab her in
the stomach and said, "This bitch is too fat it won't
go in." So she stabbed her in the chest/heart area.
Then we got our stuff and ran out the door and got
into the truck and left.

[17] *We drove to Sara's because we were scared to get*
out of the truck anywhere and we wiped off the
blood with a wet towel and asked her where we
could find some weed in the midst of Holly telling
her what just happened. I was almost speechless.

[18] *The drive to Tybee was scary as hell. I had never*
driven on the interstate before. I was shaking like I
was having a seizure, I was having hot flashes, and I
didn't even get high off the weed we smoked. I was
scared to death and my mind was blown. Holly was
kicked back in the seat like nothing happened and all
I kept saying was that we were going to prison for the
rest of our lives. But she kept saying no we're not.

[19] *I was lost in Savannah I didn't know we were in Tybee. We didn't have any cigarettes left and I was driving in circles until I seen the two boys and they were smoking so I stopped and Holly asked them for a cigarette. We then asked them what they were about to do and they said go to the beach and smoke meaning weed. We parked the truck and they asked us if we wanted to come and we were like "sure". So, we got out and walked to the beach and smoked with them. We told them we had ran away and stole the truck. We went to the boys' house to hang out for a little while. We then asked them could we stay the night cuz we didn't have anywhere else to go. We took some Adavant [Ativan] and talked for a while then I guess we fell asleep.*

[20] *The next day when we woke up one of the boys gave us some clothes to change into. Holly let her mom use her grandmother's cell phone and like maybe an hour or two later we heard the police busting in the next door neighbors' house. I looked at Holly and said "it's over." She tried to hide but there was nowhere to go. Then the police busted in the boys' house and I knew it was over so I stepped to the bedroom door and they pointed their guns at me and yelled "get on the fuckin floor" so I dropped to the floor and they ran in there and one of the men kneed my back in. Then they went over to Holly. I don't even remember if they read us our rights. They searched us and Holly tried to resist arrest. They took my shoes, my dad's pocket knife, and a kitchen knife from me and they took out car keys, the cell phone, and some jewelry from Holly.*

[21] *I told Detective Jordan every thing that happened. Everything he asked me I answered them truthfully.*

[22] *Being in jail that first night was horrible. I was having flash backs and nightmares. The girls there were asking us what happened and all I could do was cry. Holly told them that "them bitches deserved to die" and at one point made the statement that "her grandmother was too fat because she has to keep stabbing her."*

[23] *At the arraignment they told us we were charged with two counts of malice murder and 2 counts of felony murder and armed robbery* [24] *No, no! I didn't get a chance to see or talk to my parents at the arraignments.*

[25] *The adjustment to being in jail this time were harder than before because everyone was calling me a murderer, and a killer. I stayed in suicide watch for at least 2 or 3 months. I had basically given up on everything and everyone including myself. I hated myself for what happened and still do to this day.*

[26] *No! I didn't have any communication with Holly what so ever [in the months leading up to the hearings].*

[27] *I think Lloyd Walker has been good to me but at times I feel as if I was tricked into thinking I would only do 14 years and then go home.*

[28] *The memories of my sentencing were horrible. I basically gave my life away at the time of helping Holly take her grandmothers life. I feel as if I should've just asked for the death penalty because*

my life is already taken. But then I came to realize
that life in prison is better than no life at all.

[29] I do and I don't think the judge was fair. Anybody
involved in a crime like that should get what they
deserve.

[30] Do I think the sentences were fair? Yes and no. I
feel like I was tricked into my sentences. I don't feel
as if I should've got 3 concurrent life sentences. I
know what happened was beyond horrible but people have killed and only gotten 15 to 20 years and
some only a year or two.

[31] Yes I was, and am still genuinely sorry for what
happened. If I could give my life so they could live I
wouldn't think twice.

[32] I don't blame all this on Holly but I feel as if she
did influence me to help her.

[33] My stay Alto [prison] was ok. Basically, prison is
prison.

[34] I had cut myself at Alto and went to the infirmary
and when I went back to my dorm my psychiatrist
told me that if I went back to the infirmary I would
be sent to Metro. I had shaved my hair to stop from
cutting my arms and they locked me down. So, I
told them I was fixing to flip so they sent me to the
infirmary and back to Metro.

[35] Yes! I've heard from Holly. [36] I will always love
Holly but I don't feel for her anymore. I had to
bring myself to terms meaning: believing that what
your crime is, is not who you are, and I had to try to
forgive myself and I wouldn't do that and still write
to Holly. So in order for me to move forward and
stop living in the past I had to let her go. Believe me

it wasn't easy and I still miss her but it is something I had to do for me and my safety. She's just not right in the head.

[37] *I'm fixing to take my GED [General Education Degree] test in December and I'm gonna go to groups and involve myself in everything possible. I recently joined the scared straight program which is where they bring teens to the prison and we, the inmates, talk to them and try our best to scare them out of coming to prison.*

[38] *When I get out it's all about my family and me. I can't say never but I won't be looking forward to any kind of relationship. I want to be motivational speaker and talk to troubled teens all over. Cuz I feel if I can't help me maybe I can help a few of them and that means a lot to me. I also want to publish my poetry and find a worthwhile job. Believe me I wont put myself in any kind of drug related etc. situation. Drugs have really ruined my life for good and I won't turn back to it. The Devil is a liar.*

Sandra Ketchum
11/13/05

TWENTY-ONE

Holly Harvey is presently incarcerated in Pulaski State Prison in Hawkinsville, Pulaski County, Georgia, about an hour's drive south of Macon. Georgia has the fourth largest female jail population in the nation (with the ninth largest population in the country). Pulaski is a women's prison that was opened in 1994, renovated in 1998, and has an inmate population of 1,050 with a staff of 381. Approximately sixty of those prisoners are maximum security and are in isolation/segregation cells in the six-building complex. Pulaski also has a special segregated wing for juvenile offenders. Holly is just one of two juveniles in the wing, and she won't be joining the main population until she reaches the age of 17 in March 2006. Pulaski, although not on par with the notorious Alto, still houses inmates that have committed violent crimes, yet the majority of the women are in there on drug charges. Inmates have made efforts to make Pulaski homey, and flowers abound. The prison has a distinctive feminine touch to its grim surroundings.

According to her lawyer Judy Chidester, Holly's state of mind is "pretty good." She has settled in fairly well and is taking advantage of several programs the prison offers. Besides seeing a therapist to help her with anger management, she is focusing on getting her high school diploma. Chidester says that Holly has not had many visitors. Her mother, Carla, has been in to see her a few times, but because she has no driver's license and no access to a car, it has been very difficult for her to visit. But for the first time in her daughter's life, Carla has been able to give Holly some sage advice—because as she told Chidester, "I've been there." From her own time spent in prison, Carla has imparted some jailhouse wisdom, "A mixed blessing at best" Chidester said—a sad commentary on a mother–daughter relationship that was more like a friendship than familial in nature. Chidester ruminated that if Carla had not had that experience, maybe Holly wouldn't be behind bars now.

Anita Beckham is another visitor Holly will be seeing. Beckham is a friend of Carla's, and Holly lived with her during one of Carla's stints in jail. Holly often joined Beckham and her kids on summer vacation down at the shore. Beckham confessed to Chidester that she wasn't sure if she could ever go down to the beach again because it would remind her too much of the good times there with Holly, a painful burden, knowing where Holly will be for at least the next twenty years. A former teacher of Holly's has also been put on the list, and Chidester reports that there are several of the teenager's former teachers who have written her regularly and offered encouragement and support. Chidester knows this because she was given the task of screening Holly's mail, since Holly is still a juvenile. A lot of it, Chidester says, was hate mail, and weird offers of relationships from jailed adult males from as far away as Attica Prison in upstate New York.

But most important of all to Holly is that Kevin Collier has asked to be put on her visitors' list. The willingness of Kevin to visit his jailed niece buoyed Holly's spirits considerably. It was quite a reversal of feelings for the uncle who was widely quoted in the media as saying that Holly should get the death penalty for killing his parents. Chidester says Kevin told her that the first time Holly comes up for parole, he would speak in her behalf, which would have a huge impact on any parole board.

Holly has had some contact with the general prison population through supervised exercise in the prison yard, and it is Chidester's hope that she will be taken under the wing of an older, experienced woman inmate. That is usually what happens to young girls in such a potentially violent place that demands vigilance and street smarts in order to survive the often grueling humdrum of prison life.

Chidester has been able to get some of the things Holly has requested. The prison allows two magazine subscriptions per inmate that are approved by them. Holly gets *Seventeen* and *Glamour*, which she devours as soon as they arrive. One of the things Holly has learned is how to cook "prison style." Ingenuity abounds in all prisons, and Pulaski is no exception. The ingredients for the recipes at Pulaski come from an unusual source—the vending machines. Chidester says Holly was able to fashion a lemon pie from the creams between the vending machine cookies, and use soda pop to give it its lemon flavor and color.

Holly and Sandy communicated regularly by mail the first several months of their incarceration. According to Chidester such communication is allowed, since the girls' cases are over. Chidester had encouraged the correspondence. "It made Holly happy," says Chidester, improved her spirits, and helped her cope with life behind bars. The two even promised each other that they wouldn't "cut" themselves. Chidester says it is common for distraught young girls to inflict knife wounds on themselves in a form of self-punishment and a way to deal with their anguish.

Some of the things, says Chidester, that were written by the girls weren't "realistic." Sandy promised that since she is likely to get out first, that she would wait for Holly and be there at the prison when she is released, and then they could be together again. Chidester smiled at the thought and related that few adults could wait twenty years for a loved one's return, no less an impressionable teenager. Apparently Chidester was right. The correspondence trickled to just an occasional letter, and then none at all, in just four months. Since Sandy had reached the age of 17 she was now in the general prison population at Metro, which gave her the opportunity to make friends and form relationships, something Holly couldn't yet do. It was a difficult adjustment time for Holly. She had written her lawyer that she would keep one promise that Sandy and she had made. She would refrain from cutting herself.

Chidester has also encouraged Holly to write, and she has responded by penning several poems, many of which she has given to her lawyer. But Chidester is not the only one who reads her writings. Prison guards often enter her cell to search for contraband and read what she has written. It is a common practice in jail. Guards are always looking for evidence of a planned escape, even though Holly is an unlikely candidate for so risky a venture. Chidester says it has made Holly reluctant to explore her inner thoughts if they will not remain private. Her lawyer says that much of what Holly writes is "dark in nature," an understandable tone considering her predicament.

Holly hasn't quite come to terms with what she did, and that concerns Chidester. Holly will eventually have to realize the enormity and finality of her crimes. The full weight of the murders and the anguish that they caused, not only for her, but her family and friends as well, will have to be dealt with. The process of getting her to grasp what she has done started when her lawyer showed her the most gruesome crime photos from the 400 she had received from the prosecution prior to Holly's plea deal. It had been the deciding moment for the teenager to accept the deal. She, as Chidester had hoped, did not want a jury, family, and friends to see the horrible thing she had caused, and was convinced that the only realistic option was to take DA Scott Ballard's generous offer. Even though it was a traumatic and difficult thing for Holly to see the graphic photos, it was necessary, says Chidester, to start her on the road to reality. The fact that Sandy had agreed to testify against her in a trial also forced her hand.

Holly, in her meetings with her lawyer post-hearing, still says she doesn't understand why she stabbed her beloved grandparents to death. The drugs Holly used on August 2, 2004, says Chidester, definitely were a huge influence on her actions, but as she tried to explain to Holly, drugs were not a mitigating factor in the eyes of the law. Holly had confessed to her that, after she'd inflicted the first knife wound on Sarah Collier, she couldn't stop, that a force had taken hold of her. Holly didn't even have an idea on how long the murderous attacks had taken. It could have been five minutes or thirty—she had no concept of time. Holly told Chidester that she would have thought her grandparents would have cried out, but the only screaming she remembers came from her.

Chidester is convinced that if Holly had gone to trial, she would have been convicted and be looking at a minimum of 38 years behind bars before she would be eligible for parole, as opposed to the 20 years the prosecution was offering. "It was," she says, "a good deal for Holly."

There was another factor for Fayette County in negotiating the deal Holly had gotten. It has been estimated that it would have cost the county over $400,000 to bring the girls to trial in distant and remote Thomasville, Georgia. The prosecution had a witness list of over sixty people, and would have had to provide hotel rooms for all of them for the length of the trial, which could have gone on for two weeks. Fayette County would have had to bring their own security, which would have stretched the sheriff's department's resources, most notably in the manpower they employed to police their county.

Chidester is still bitter about how her client was portrayed in the media as "a stone-cold remorseless killer." That was, according to the lawyer, due in large part to Lieutenant Colonel Bruce Jordan and his willingness to appear in front of cameras and condemn Holly—but not Sandy, because she had cooperated immediately with police.

Another thing that irked Holly's lawyer was how her client was demonized in the media as unremorseful at the time of her arrest. Holly, in fact, was very remorseful and scared, Chidester says. She became "the evil one" because she exercised her legal right to keep quiet until she had an attorney's counsel. Holly told her that she and Sandy were hysterical and distraught once they realized what they had done that night, sitting in Carl Collier's truck after the murders. They were shaking so much that it took several minutes of trying before they could get the key into the ignition and start the car. Lloyd Walker confirmed the story to Chidester, because Sandy, his client, had told him the same thing.

It is Judy Chidester's fear that Holly—and she—will never be able to find the answer as to why she killed her grandparents.

"I don't know if there is one. Even if her grandparents had been awful to Holly and done bad things to her—and there were times when the religious couple had been cruel to her— [it] still couldn't justify Holly's murderous act."

Chidester pored over Holly's school records from first grade on up. She also studied her past brushes with the law, and there was no red flag, nothing that might have indicated that the murders were predictable. The horrific killings of the Colliers seem to have come out of nowhere. The fact that the crime was committed by young girls makes the case even more unfathomable. The public has been hardened to violent crimes by young males, but felonies by post-pubescent girls have rattled the consciousness of the nation—hence the fascination this case holds. Chidester adds that the public has a naïve view of what's going on in the minds of young people. They don't understand that the notion of youthful innocence doesn't seem to apply anymore.

Judy Chidester believes she will see less and less of Holly over the coming years, and there may be a time in the future when their communication will end altogether. But, she says, she will always sadly and fondly remember Holly and the case that rocked the tranquil communities of Fayette County.